Behavioural Worlds

Behavioural Worlds

THE STUDY OF SINGLE CASES

P. G. HERBST

TAVISTOCK PUBLICATIONS

LONDON · SYDNEY · TORONTO · WELLINGTON

First published in 1970
by Tavistock Publications Limited
11 New Fetter Lane, London EC4
SBN 422 73260 5

Printed in Great Britain
By Willmer Brothers Limited, Birkenhead

First published as a Social Science Paperback in 1973
SBN 422 75550 8

Distributed in the USA
by Harper & Row Publishers, Inc.
Barnes & Noble Import Division

Ex omnibus partibus relucit totum

The all shines out from every individual.

NICHOLAS OF CUSA
(15th century AD)

The most ordinary beings are profoundly holy.

HUI HAI
(9th century AD)

CONTENTS

PART III

ANALYSIS OF COGNITIVE AND SOCIAL STRUCTURES

PREFACE

SYSTEMATIC AND quantitative studies of behaviour have in the past been almost exclusively based on data obtained from population samples. As a result, it has been difficult to determine whether, or to what extent, the hypotheses and theories tested are applicable to individual persons or groups. Also, the results obtained have been of only limited help to the psychologist or social scientist who in his daily work is concerned with gaining an understanding of a particular person, group, or organization.

This book reports the experience gained over the past fifteen years in the exploratory development of four different types of technique for studying single cases, which have been applied to the investigation of autonomous group functioning, to pupil-task relationships at school, to family process analysis, and to organizational behaviour. The basic characteristics of each technique are shown in *Table 1*.

If the results obtained in these studies should come to have implications for the future development of the behavioural sciences then this will in the first place be due to the findings reported in Chapters 8 and 9, which show that the principles of human behaviour are not necessarily universal but can vary from case to case. Some of the fundamental assumptions which have provided the basis for behaviour theories therefore need to be taken up for reconsideration.

Although it was not always clearly realized, the basic assumptions for both psychological and sociological theories were taken over by analogy from classical physics. Insufficient attention was paid to the fact that a theory of physics cannot serve as a general model for scientific method. The theory of physics has to account for the special characteristics of physical phenomena, and these differ fundamentally from those encountered in the study of human behaviour.

TABLE 1 TECHNIQUES FOR STUDYING SINGLE CASES

Technique	Chapter	Basic data	Type of measure	Type of analysis
Longitudinal time-independent	6	Quantitative	External physicalist	Functional network analysis
Cross-sectional	7, 8, 9	Quantitative	Subjective intensity and probability scale	Functional network analysis
Longitudinal phase-transition	10, 11	Qualitative	Frequency based on content analysis	Topometric structure analysis, percentage frequencies, and cumulative frequency trajectories
Longitudinal time-dependent	14	Quantitative	External physicalist	Markoff process network analysis

In physics it was possible to start off with the assumption that there exists a single universe within which the same set of laws and the same measurement scales apply everywhere and do not change over time. The fact that even in physics these assumptions had to be modified around the turn of the century, when it was found that physical principles can differ according to the size of unit studied and that, under certain conditions, measurement scales expand or contract, may make it easier to accept that properties of this kind, instead of being unusual, turn out to be essential characteristics of human behaviour.

What is found is that every person and every group has the characteristics of a behavioural universe which evolves its own laws and measurement scales. Further, it is almost certain that even for the same person or group the principles of behaviour can change over time.

I had started off with the expectation that it would be possible on the basis of general system theoretical concepts to formulate a theory of behaviour applicable to all persons and groups. Examination of case after case obtained in the pupil-task study led to the abandonment of this belief. It was not possible to find even a pair of children for whom the interrelationship of behaviour variables could be regarded as similar. It is true that, if the data for a class of children are summed together, a stable pattern of relationships between behaviour variables emerges. However, the results obtained in this way bear no relation to the pattern of relationships found for any individual child. This leaves the problem of how data obtained by population-sample studies can be interpreted. The indications are that they refer to properties of populations but not necessarily to characteristics of individual human behaviour.

It appeared at this stage that the only alternative would be to construct a different behaviour theory for every human being. I began initially to work on the data obtained for one child for whom all the relationships between behaviour variables were of a relatively simple type, and then added further cases which satisfied necessary conditions for quantitative case-study analysis. While it was possible to formulate possible networks of behaviour principles for each case examined, it was clearly impossible to go very far without a foundation to work on.

What was needed was at least a set of basic working principles which would make it possible to construct the different types of networks of behaviour principles that were found to exist. This immediately suggested the idea that there might be certain constant and invariant characteristics which apply to all behaviour principles that can come into operation, and also that there might exist invariant characteristics which apply to all possible transformations of measurement scales. If so, then it would after all be possible to arrive at a general behaviour theory applicable to both persons and groups, but, unlike physics, where what is invariant at least within limits is the relationship between physical variables, in behaviour theory, invariance would be found to exist at the level of construction rules for the possible behaviour principles that can come into operation.

The construction rules for possible behaviour principles can be put in the form of two postulates which are discussed in Chapter 3. In Chapter 6 it is shown how the postulates can be applied to the derivation of a set of behaviour principles previously obtained in a study of autonomous group functioning, and in Chapters 8 and 9 it is shown that the same postulates make it possible to derive the networks of behaviour principles found in the pupil-task study.

The application of the postulates presupposes that, for any given case, the linkage of variables in the behaviour network is known. In Chapter 4 an empirical method is described which, under certain conditions, makes it possible to determine the location of variables in a behaviour network.

Chapters 10 and 11 describe a longitudinal method for analysing autobiographical data obtained in interviews. The technique was applied to the analysis of joint interviews of an engaged couple over the period of a year, beginning with the period when they first met and ending with the period during which the wedding arrangements were made. It is possible in this case to study in detail the structural evolution of both the interpersonal relationships and the external relationships of the couple as seen from the point of view of each partner.

The process of structural evolution is found to go through clearly demarcated transitional phases. Critical transition boundaries separate each phase of the interpersonal relationship structure from the succeeding one. What one is dealing with here is successive steps leading to increased mutual commitment, and in the final chapter this process is analysed in a quantitative form, this time in the context of labour turnover studies.

What all the longitudinal case-study techniques show is that the process of structural development is not continuous, but that both persons and groups go through phases during which a steady state of structural characteristics of the behaviour system is maintained followed by a more or less abrupt transition to a different relationship structure. If a steady state is achieved of the internal and the transactional parameters of the behaviour network, then a stable set of behaviour principles emerges and can be identified.

The fact that the general form of measurement-scale transformations is found to be of a projective type indicates that it will eventually be possible to discard the use of algebras based on Cartesian geometry in favour of algebras based on the properties of a projective space. This would mean that neither behaviour theory nor measurement would need to depend on quantitative information. While there is no difficulty in transforming the behaviour principles discussed into a projective algebraic form, what is lacking at present is a technique for plotting and fitting data in a projective space and criteria for constructing suitable types of measurement scale. Although this may not have immediate practical implications for studies based on external physicalist measurement scales, the development of techniques based on projective geometry may provide a better solution for problems encountered in studies based on subjective scales.

Over the past five years, most of the research reported was supported by means of an unspecified research grant from the

Norwegian Council for Science and the Humanities. I am deeply grateful for this privilege, and for the kindness and support of Dosent Einar Thorsrud, Director during this period of the Institute for Industrial Social Research, Trondheim, and later of the Work Research Institutes, Oslo. I wish to thank Dr Rhona Rapoport for permission to use the case-study material discussed in Chapters 10 and 11, and I am grateful that I had the opportunity of working with her as consultant on a family research project at Harvard University School of Public Health. I am indebted to Dr F. E. Emery for permission to use, in the chapter on sense modalities, material originally written as a consultancy report for a project which he directed at the Human Resources Centre of the Tavistock Institute of Human Relations. Last, and by no means least, my thanks again to Toril Hungnes for her untiring secretarial help.

P. G. Herbst

Trondheim, 1968

PART ONE

Generalized Behaviour Theory

CHAPTER 1

The Range of Possible Behavioural Laws and Research Methodology

———◆———

SUMMARY

The development of the behavioural sciences has been handicapped in the past by the use of classical physics as a scientific model. Classical physics was based on laws characterized by invariant functional relationships and constant parameters. In the case of behavioural organizations neither the functional relationship between behaviour variables nor parameters are necessarily invariant or constant. A different type of approach to the construction of methods and theory is therefore required in the study of human behaviour.

———◆———

THE ESSENTIAL concern of science is the search for invariance in phenomena; the search within the constant flux of change for what is unchanging and eternal, for that which can be absolutely relied on. Science, however, is not primarily concerned with analysing the direct experience of phenomena, but with the analysis of a conceptual representation of phenomena. A scientific law is a statement of a specific type of invariance in the conceptual representation of phenomena.

The choice we make in the representation of phenomena is therefore a crucial step in the development of a scientific theory. If we choose one form of representation, relationships between phenomena will appear complex and confused, and no comprehensible laws may emerge. This, I think, appears to be a fair description of the present state of the behavioural sciences. However, if we find a better representation, the relationships between phenomena may emerge as simple and comprehensible,

3

and a whole range of invariant relationships may then easily be formulated in the form of laws.

This is what has happened in the development of the theory of physics and most clearly in the field of astronomy. Given the Ptolemaic system, the paths of the planets appeared incomprehensible and fantastic and so were the theoretical models needed to account for them. With the change of representation introduced by Copernicus, the paths of the planets turned out to have a simple cyclic-type form. Within a short time we find that Kepler was able to formulate the laws of planetary motion and Newton was able to develop his general theory, and it is at this point that physics as a science began.

The basic problem that faces us in the behavioural sciences is, I think, just this: the search for a workable representation of behavioural phenomena. In a formal sense a new form of representation means the introduction of a new set of basic axioms or postulates, and these postulates will inevitably be different from those of physics. For if we use the same set of postulates as in physics, all we can potentially deduce from them are physical laws and not behavioural laws. In time, it will become possible to provide a closer integration of the physical and the behavioural sciences. However, before we can build a bridge, we need to have reasonably firm foundations on both sides.

The systematic empirical study of human behaviour is nearly a hundred years old. During this time remarkably little progress has been made in the way of finding generally accepted laws. The question that may be asked is why this is the case.

There are at least three possibilities. The first one is that as far as human behaviour is concerned no universal principles of any kind can be formulated. This is a conclusion which cannot be ruled out, but which it would be premature to adopt until all other alternatives have been examined. The two remaining possibilities are:

1. The laws of behaviour are of a different type from those we have been looking for up to now.

4

2. The methods at present in use are not adequate for discovering behavioural laws.

Now clearly the type of method we use depends very much on the type of principle we expect to discover. So, before we can decide on the proper methods to use, we need to have some idea of what kinds of behavioural law we can expect to find. Here, the experience gained in past studies will be of use at least in so far as it can help us, on the basis of accumulated experience, to get some idea of the types of law that are unlikely to apply in the field of human behaviour.

The possible kinds of law are definable in terms of their invariance properties.

TYPE A LAW

Both the functional form of the relationship and parametric values are universal constants.

An example is the gas law

$$\frac{pv}{T} = R$$

which states that if we multiply the pressure p with the volume v of a given mass of gas and divide by the absolute temperature T then (within a given range of these variables) we will always obtain the same value R, which is the gas constant. In this case, then, both the functional relationship and the parameter R are constants.

One way of testing this relationship might be to take a random sample of gases, and to mix them all together, and if we did this we would in fact be able to confirm the relationship. However, this would not be the best method to use. What we would normally do is to take just one gas at a time in order to confirm that the functional relationship is in fact the same for each gas. Next, we would estimate the value of the parameter R to find out whether this value is in fact identical for every gas we may choose.

The important characteristic of a Type A law is that if we were to use a population-sample technique we would be able to discover this type of functional law. However, if the law is not of this type, then population-study techniques will be quite inappropriate or altogether useless. If there is a conclusion to be drawn from half a century of population-study techniques, it is that the existence of a Type A law is highly improbable as far as the behavioural sciences are concerned. However, even in physics only a limited number of relationships have this level of invariance, and many are of a weaker type.[1]

TYPE B LAW

The functional form of the relationship is a universal constant but parameters are specific.

An example from physics is the law which gives the rate of expansion of a metal rod with temperature. If L is the length of the rod and T the absolute temperature, then

$$L = cT$$

The parameter c is a specific constant for each metal. The functional form of the relationship is the same for all metals but, depending on the value c, the rate of expansion differs for different metals. Behavioural laws of this type appear to be a very real possibility. The law would have the same form in each case but the parameters would have different values for different persons and groups. The only modification we should need to make is that parameters would not necessarily be fixed. Instead, depending on the extent to which a given situation becomes structured, parameters acquire a steady-state value, and if the situation is restructured parameters can acquire a new steady-state value. We will need to be prepared in this case

---

[1] The study of individual gases does in fact show that the gas constant has the same value only for gases of the same molecular weight. In order to obtain a universal gas constant R_0, therefore, the specific molecular weight has to be introduced into the equation, so that not even the gas law is a perfect Type A law. It is interesting to speculate whether, if physicists had restricted themselves to the use of statistical techniques, the development of the physical sciences would have become possible.

to find situations which are so unstructured that no simple behaviour principles emerge.

Before going on to consider the possibility of laws with even weaker invariance conditions, we need to be quite clear about what are the empirical implications of a Type B law. Let us take as a simple example the relationship

$$y = \alpha x$$

where α is a parameter. Depending on whether α is positive, zero, or negative, an increase in x will increase y, have no effect on y, or decrease y.

What is tested in the case of a Type B law is that the functional relationship is always of the same form, in this case a linear form. This is clearly different from the type of hypothesis normally tested in behavioural research, which assumes that the relationship is positive, zero, or negative. Furthermore, if population-sample techniques are employed, we would, even if a law existed, be unable to discover it, and we would arrive at a zero correlation, except where, owing to differences in the populations sampled, some studies would be able to demonstrate a positive or a negative correlation. Unless, then, we expect to find a Type A law, it becomes essential to base hypothesis-testing on the study of individual cases. Moreover,

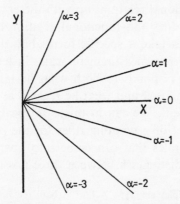

FIGURE 1 LINEAR TYPE B LAW
The relationship can be positive or negative

7

the situation will need to be one that has acquired a stable structure so that parametric steady-state conditions are maintained; and, finally, the technique should be one that does not disturb the parametric values.

There are at present indications that there might be some Type B laws in the field of human behaviour. Many behaviour principles do not, however, appear to be of this type either. Now, as far as physics is concerned, if a law is neither of Type A nor of Type B form, then we do not have a law at all.[1] In order to construct a behavioural science, therefore, we need to go outside the traditional region of theory construction and look for a deeper level of invariance.

TYPE C LAW

Both the functional relationship and parameters are specific, but the generating rules for possible functional relationships are a universal constant.

The existence of Type C laws implies that each person and each group constitutes a behavioural universe which operates on the basis of its own laws. In so far as these laws can change over time in the course of development they have to be looked at as self-created and as emergent from an existing system structure and the transactional relationship with the environment. However, not only does the functional relationship between behaviour variables take a specific form; but also every person operates on his own measurement scales in terms of which he experiences and responds to both what he takes to belong to and be part of himself and what he regards as relevant aspects of his environment. We can in this case speak of laws only if we can find a set of generating rules for the possible range of behaviour principles that can come into operation.

We can thus distinguish between three possible types of law

[1] Stochastic principles are Type A laws if both the functional relationship and the probability parameter are universal constants. They are Type B laws either if the probability parameter is specific or if the probability parameter changes according to a determinate principle.

in terms of invariance properties. Of these, Types A and B fall within the range of physical theory and Types B and C are those which we may expect to fall within the range of behaviour theory.

Type	Invariant	
A	Functional form and parameters	} Physical theory
B	Functional form	
C	Postulates which generate possible functional forms	} Behaviour theory

We have seen that, except in the case of Type A laws, useful results cannot as a rule be expected from population-sample studies. As far as behavioural research is concerned these methods are appropriate only when we are interested in the study of populations rather than of single individuals or groups; they are also appropriate in operational research where we may be seeking to optimize population characteristics. For the testing of individual behaviour principles, however, population-study techniques are inappropriate. They may have some use in preliminary exploratory research, but whatever results are obtained will always need to be confirmed by systematic testing at the level of individual cases.

CONTROL VERSUS MEASUREMENT TECHNIQUES

Since the chance of finding Type A laws in behavioural research is remote, the possibility of testing any form of behaviour theory requires the development of techniques for studying individual cases.

Here we have a choice between two possible techniques, of which the most familiar is the *controlled experiment technique*. This is the type of technique that was originally used in the testing of the gas law.

The procedure in this case is to keep, say, the pressure constant, and to set the temperature at 0, 10, 20 ... degrees and then plot the temperature against the measured volume. Next we can keep the volume constant, again vary the temperature, and then plot the temperature against the measured pressure obtained. In each case we would get a linear relationship.

However, there is a much simpler non-experimental method that can be used, which can be referred to as the *multivariate measurement technique*. What we do in this case is take successive measures of all three variables, and we obtain a table as follows:

Time 1	Time 2	Time 3	
p_1	p_2	p_3	$\cdots$
v_1	v_2	v_3	$\cdots$
T_1	T_2	T_3	$\cdots$

We then calculate the ratios

$$\frac{p_1 v_1}{T_1}, \quad \frac{p_2 v_2}{T_2}, \quad \frac{p_3 v_3}{T_3}$$

and we confirm, with far less trouble, that the values obtained are the same constant value R in each case.

We may then ask why this simpler method has rarely been employed in physics. The main reason is that, as far as physics is concerned, the method would not normally be efficient since the natural ranges of variation in pressure, volume, and temperature are quite small. The laboratory technique made it possible to create extreme conditions of pressure, and temperatures that are not found under natural conditions, so that the full range of the law could be tested. In behavioural research the position is generally quite the reverse. The full range of behaviour variables is found under natural conditions, so that there is as a rule no need to attempt to create extreme conditions artificially.

However, there are other reasons as well why experimental manipulation techniques based on the techniques developed in the physical sciences are not necessarily valid or appropriate in behavioural research. In behavioural research we are not in a position to satisfy those conditions that made controlled experimentation possible in the physical sciences:

1. We cannot set relevant variables such as interest, stress, or anxiety at given quantitative values such as 10, 20, 30. In fact we cannot even create a standard condition under which different persons would all experience even qualitatively some degree of interest, stress, or anxiety. If we did want to do this, we would need to create *different* conditions for each person. Even then we could not set and maintain any of these variables at a given quantitative level, and we are thus unable to generate the data required for quantitative theory testing.

2. We cannot control variables better than we can measure them; in fact we can always measure far more precisely than we can control. Even under the best conditions we cannot hope to approach the measurement precision of the physical sciences. Since accurate behavioural measurement is quite difficult and the control of behaviour variables is necessarily even less precise, we introduce unnecessarily additional unreliability. We need to except here physically definable constraints deriving from the task structure, since these can be adequately controlled.

3. In the case of the gas laws, where controlled experimentation is not only the appropriate but also the optimal technique, we have a condition where the state of the system is completely definable in terms of three variables. In the study of behavioural organizations we have to deal with larger networks of behaviour variables. In order to map out the structure of networks of variables we require simultaneous quantitative measures of several variables.

Any type of law is testable only under ideal conditions, and what is ideal depends on the characteristics of the phenomena studied. We often seem to forget that physical laws are testable only under quite specific, ideal conditions which are often very difficult to satisfy. Who would venture to predict the path of a feather on a windy day? Or, if this seems too difficult, suppose we construct a perfectly round billiard table, and a perfectly round ball. We now set the ball off on a given trajectory and with given velocity. We would expect that, given the known laws of mechanics, the path of the ball would be predictable. In fact it is completely unpredictable. The slightest imperfection may set the ball rolling off on a different path which then becomes amplified. And if the experiment is repeated a different path may be obtained every time. It seems curious then, in view of the extremely restricted conditions under which physical laws hold, that when we turn to behavioural research it is expected that behavioural laws can be tested on persons selected at random and with little systematic analysis of the ideal conditions which need to be at least approximately satisfied.

A necessary condition for stable behavioural relationships to manifest themselves is that parametric steady-state conditions are firmly established and maintained. Ideal conditions of this type can be found under everyday conditions where persons have built up a stable cognitive and behavioural structure. We know that if a person starts a new job or becomes a member of a new organization it generally takes weeks and often months before these conditions are achieved.

For testing behaviour principles, laboratory experiments provide in this respect almost the least suitable conditions that could be devised. The subject is precipitated for a short period of time into a situation which for him is both highly unstructured and ambiguous. It is ambiguous for him in terms of his expectations of what the experiment is about, in terms of the instruction and setting with which he is presented, and in terms of the kind of behaviour required of him to please his professor so that he can pass his course or to earn the monetary reward offered; and, last but not least, it is ambiguous owing to the more or less transparent deception to which he is submitted.

It is here that we come to the crucial problem in the use of behavioural laboratory techniques. Is it reasonable to assume that truth can be arrived at by means of deception? However effectively or ineffectively we manipulate behaviour in the laboratory setting, we can scarcely do so without using deception. At the same time, the possibility of obtaining reliable data is dependent entirely on the honesty, trust, and cooperation of the subjects involved. By using deception as a systematic technique the experimenter destroys the very basis required for behavioural research. Deception leads to counter-deception, and trust once lost can scarcely ever be regained.

Bronowski (1959) writes:

'Whatever else may be held against science this cannot be denied, that it takes for its ultimate judgement one criteria alone, that it shall be truthful.'

and Schrödinger (1958):

'The scientist only imposes two things namely truth and sincerity, imposes them on himself and upon other scientists.'

What both writers in their discussion of the physical sciences point to is that, in scientific research, ethics is not a matter of choice or convenience, but the essential core and the basis on which science itself rests. In the behavioural sciences, where we are concerned not with objects or even subjects but with human beings, a commitment to honesty will not be sufficient as an ethical basis, but without it no science can develop and maintain itself.

The main task for behavioural science at present will need to be the search for and development of research techniques which, in addition to being technically sound, satisfy basic ethical criteria. In the behavioural even more than in the physical sciences these two requirements are by no means inconsistent; indeed, they are intimately related to one another.

CHAPTER 2

The Breakdown of Physicalist Postulates in Behaviour Theory

————◆————

SUMMARY

If the postulates of classical physics are applied to the behavioural sciences then we are led to suppose that a universally valid behaviour theory can be formulated and that invariant measurement scales can be constructed. The results obtained by means of quantitative case-study techniques show that neither of these conditions applies in the behavioural sciences.

Both the relationships between behaviour variables and the measurement scales on which behaviour is based are found to differ from case to case. Every person and every group therefore has to be looked at as a behavioural universe with its own laws and measurement scales.

————◆————

IN THE attempts that have been made to develop a behavioural science, a number of basic assumptions were taken over from classical physics. The assumptions made in classical physics may be set out as follows:

1. A uniform set of laws exists which applies to the total physical universe and to every one of its sub-units.
2. Measurement scales can be constructed which will give invariant readings irrespective of the object to which they are applied, the time of measurement, and the part of the physical universe in which they are applied.

The corresponding assumptions that have been made in the behavioural sciences can then be put as follows:

14

1. A uniform set of behaviour principles can be formulated which applies to all persons and groups respectively.
2. Measurement scales can be constructed which will measure the same behavioural variable both qualitatively and quantitatively when applied to different persons or groups.

A test of these assumptions required the development of techniques for the quantitative study of individual cases. So far two such techniques have been constructed. The first of these is the multivariate longitudinal case-study technique, based on the existence of a repeated task-cycle unit. A necessary condition for this method is that parametric steady-state conditions are achieved and maintained, so that successive measures can be taken to represent different states of the same behaviour system. The alternative method used in more recent research is the multivariate cross-sectional case-study technique. This is based on the simultaneous measurement of different ongoing independent tasks which form part of the same total situation. Here the necessary condition is that the same parametric conditions apply to each task, so that again the measures obtained can be taken to represent different states of the same behaviour system.

THE LONGITUDINAL TECHNIQUE

The basic model of the longitudinal case-study technique is as follows. Given a person or group with a repetitive task-cycle unit, which can be measured in terms of a set of variables x, y, z . . ., which are representative of the same task unit and representative of the total cycle unit, a set of measures

$$(x_1 y_1 z_1 \ldots), (x_2 y_2 z_2 \ldots), \ldots (x_n y_n z_n \ldots)$$

for successive cycle units is obtained. Provided parametric steady-state conditions are maintained, then the sequence of cycle units can be disregarded. The measures in this case constitute different possible states of the same system, and the data can be plotted in a three-variable phase-space to determine functional relationships.

This method was applied in the study of a small autonomous working group in a British coalmine (Herbst, 1962). The work team controlled both its input and its output, and its internal functioning. Since in this case none of the variables of group functioning was externally controlled, a group of this type provided an ideal study object. Measurement was based on a continuous task-allocation record maintained by the team over a three-month period. The group task consisted of a repetitive work-cycle which took three to five days to complete. A set of seven measures was obtained for each cycle unit.

It took the group about one and a half weeks of working together until parameters of group functioning were stabilized at steady-state values, so that for the subsequent period a network of functional relationships between variables of group functioning emerged, which could be formulated and tested. The network of functional relationships was in this case concerned with a condition of outcome predictability, which may be defined as a situation where the output rate of the system is predictable as a function of the rate of operation of activity elements that form part of the system and of the degree of integration of activity processes.

The study of this one group took about five years to carry out from the time the data became available, and although with the basic techniques developed less time would now be required, it would still take a long time before a reasonably large number of longitudinal case-studies could be completed. The next step was therefore to see whether it would be possible to construct an alternative technique which would provide quantitative case-study material for a larger number of cases in a shorter period.

THE CROSS-SECTIONAL TECHNIQUE

The basic model of what may be called the cross-sectional case-study technique is as follows. We start off with a set of different tasks carried out by the same person or group under similar conditions. If all such tasks are measured simultaneously in terms of a set of variables $(x, y, z \ldots)$, then for each task we obtain a set of measures $(x_1 y_1 z_1 \ldots) \ldots (x_n y_n z_n \ldots)$. Provided that the same parametric values apply to all the tasks the set of measures can be treated as different possible states of the same system. The data can then be plotted in a three-variable phase-space to determine functional relationships.

It may be noted that specific characteristics associated with tasks will appear as parameters in the longitudinal technique but as variables in the cross-sectional technique. Further, whereas the longitudinal case-study is limited by the number of successive cycle units during which parametric steady-state conditions are maintained, the cross-sectional technique is limited by the number of different tasks carried out to which identical parametric values apply.

This method has been applied to the study of pupil-task relationships at school. For each of a set of subjects taken, such as English, mathematics, religion, measures were obtained of:

1. The amount of work the pupil allocated to the subject
2. The amount of work he judged to be required to obtain a satisfactory grade
3. The boredom he experienced with the work for the subject
4. The examination grade he expected to get in the subject
5. Uncertainty about the expected grade
6. The level of anxiety about examination results in the subject.

The age-range selected was that at which pupils take, during the school year, a maximum number of subjects. In Norwegian schools this is in the ninth grade, where pupils take ten different subjects. If in this case a pupil uses examination grades as the relevant outcome criteria, then the situation is one of outcome uncertainty, since no functional relationship exists that will predict the examination grade received as a function of the amount of work invested and skill employed during the preceding study period. For each pupil the data were plotted using three-variable graphs. Concentrating in the first place on pupils for whom all the variable plots were of a relatively simple functional form, it was found that, while for a few three-variable plots similar functional relationships emerged, no two persons had a similar set of functional relationships for the twenty variable plots obtained for the six variables. Thus the network of functional relationships between behaviour variables that applies to one pupil does not necessarily apply to other pupils. The assumption that the behaviour of different persons conforms to the same specific behaviour principles had to be rejected at this stage.

EXTERNAL AND SUBJECTIVE MEASUREMENT SCALES

The assumption that a measurement scale applied to one person or group will measure the same thing when applied to another person or group will need to be considered with respect to both external and subjective scales.

Let us consider first the external scales used in the group study which was based on objective work-record data. It was found in this case that amount of time lost owing to technical breakdowns constituted aim interference and operated as a measure of stress. However, for a different group, time lost may not be aim-interfering and may be responded to as a desirable event. Even if, for two groups, work interference operates as stress, the scale may differ quantitatively both with respect to its zero point and with respect to interval distances, so that different amounts of time lost correspond to different amounts of stress experienced.

It may look as if this problem could be overcome by obtaining direct subjective measures instead; however, this is not the case. For suppose we employ an intensity rating-scale of the kind 'none, somewhat, very, extremely' to obtain information about how much work is carried out on different school subjects. If two persons A and B give the information that they work 'very' hard on mathematics, we cannot tell whether A works harder on mathematics than B, the same amount as B, or less than B. The subjective scales are thus similar to external scales, since they vary both in the operative zero point and in interval size for different persons.

The major difference between subjective and external scales is that, in the former, the variables are defined from the start, and we assume that different persons can identify experiential states such as boredom, anxiety, or work effort at least qualitatively in the same way. In the case of external scales based on behaviour-recording we do not know from the start which recorded measures of behaviour and outcome operate for a particular person (or group) as measures of performance, work effort, or stress. The external measures have in this case to be transformed into the measurement scales in terms of which the specific person or group operates.

On the whole, since external measures can almost always be constructed with far stronger scale properties than subjective measures, and to the extent that quantitative scale-transformations are definable, the longitudinal case-study approach based on external measurement may well be preferred. However, external measurement cannot be used for variables such as performance satisfaction, boredom experienced, etc.

The cross-sectional technique involves the use of rather weaker scales. However, in so far as quantitative models are testable by means of ordinal scales, which will contain most of the behaviourally relevant information, this may not matter too much. The main advantage of this method is the possibility that it provides of obtaining a large amount of quantitative case-study material in a short time.

With respect to external scales it is found that we cannot assume that a measurement scale of this type will have the same metric properties when it is applied to the behavioural measurement of different persons or groups. We cannot even assume that it will measure qualitatively the same behavioural variable.

With respect to subjective scales, we may under suitable conditions be able to measure the same behavioural characteristic. However, as in the case of external scales, the metrical

C

properties of subjective scales will differ for different persons or groups. Classical physics operated on the assumption that measurement scales could be constructed which remained invariant when applied to different objects and invariant over time. In the behavioural sciences this is not the case. Our measurement scales when applied to different behavioural organizations can expand, contract, change their interval distance and zero point, and, in the case of external scales, reverse themselves. A measurement scale will not even remain invariant when applied to the same behavioural organization at different time-periods, except in so far as parametric steady-state conditions are maintained.

TOWARDS A GENERALIZED BEHAVIOUR THEORY

Analysis of both the measurement conditions and the available quantitative case-study material shows that every person and every group has to be looked at as a behavioural universe which operates in terms of its own specific behavioural laws and on the basis of its own measurement scales.

Neither the laws nor the measurement scales that operate in the case of a given behaviour system remain unchanged over time. However, over a given time-period, parametric steady-state properties can exist, so that, during this period, behavioural laws and measurement scales remain unchanged.

It looked at this stage as if the formulation of any kind of general behaviour theory either in psychology or in sociology might be impossible. However, if we have come to the point where the problem is stated correctly, then there exists at least a possibility of solving it or of showing on logical grounds that no solution exists.

To begin with, in the cross-sectional case-study, the network of functional relationships was formulated for a number of pupils for whom the relationship between variables was of a relatively simple type. Since in each case a different network of relationships was found, this meant in fact that a different behaviour theory had to be worked out for every single case.

The question that then presented itself was whether there might be a generalized behaviour theory from which each of the empirically found networks of functional relationships could be derived as a special case. I tried at first an inductive procedure. However, this does not turn out to be feasible. For any given set of cases many different sets of generalized functional relation networks can be constructed from which each individual network is derivable as a special case. Since, with each additional case that does not fit, a new generalized set of equations will have to be constructed, and, to make matters even worse, since for each individual case alternative functional relation networks may be feasible, this seems like an endless task.

There was at least one alternative possibility that remained. Suppose that, instead of starting off with individual cases in order to work out a generalized theory, we start off, so to say, from the opposite end. Every behaviour system, we said, has its unique sets of laws. However, behaviour variables cannot be connected in any way whatsoever. Suppose, then, that we can formulate the constraints that must apply in every case with respect to the way in which behaviour variables can be connected; we can thus exclude all relationships that cannot be empirically realized, while the remainder will be the laws that can operate in all the possible kinds of behavioural universe that may evolve, which is the solution we are looking for.

CHAPTER 3

Postulates of Generalized Behaviour Theory

———◆———

SUMMARY

The aim in theory construction is the formulation of those characteristics in a given field of phenomena that remain invariant universally and over time. In physics these invariances emerged at the level of laws, which state the relationships among physical variables. At the same time, to the extent that invariance properties could be assumed for measurement scales, a basis existed for the determination of universal parametric constants. In the study of human behaviour the relationships between behaviour variables are generally neither universal nor invariant over time, nor do psychological measurement scales possess these properties. What we need to do in this case is to look for invariance properties at a more fundamental level. What we will arrive at is not a universal set of behaviour principles but a set of postulates which are able to generate the possible behavioural universes that can evolve and to exclude those that cannot come into being. Since variations can occur both in individual behaviour principles and in the measurement scales in terms of which each behaviour system operates, at least two postulates will be required:

Postulate 1, which specifies the possible structural relationships that can exist between behaviour variables, and
Postulate 2, which specifies the possible transformations of behavioural measurement scales.

———◆———

WE STARTED off by noting that each person can evolve a behavioural universe with its own network of behaviour principles. However, there are certain limitations on the form this network can take. To give an analogy: with a set of bricks, we can build a large variety of structures; however, we cannot build any structure whatsoever. Constraints exist owing to the nature of the bricks, which limits the possible ways in which they can be joined together. When a relationship is set up between behaviour variables, the equal sign requires that both sides of the equation have the same dimension. The content of the first postulate thus has to be a specification of a set of dimensions for behaviour variables together with an operational criterion for identifying the dimension of different behaviour variables.

The method of dimensional analysis is perhaps one of the most powerful techniques that have been developed; it was used originally by Newton, who referred to it as the principle of similitude. Given nothing else but the dimension of physical variables, a correct law which relates any given set of physical variables can be constructed. However, the method has never been fully formalized and it contains a special assumption, namely that any one variable is expressible as the product of powers of other variables.[1] We cannot assume that this special assumption will necessarily hold for the relationship between behaviour variables.

Let us now turn to the second postulate that is needed. Each behaviour variable is subject to change owing to changes in the measurement scales in terms of which the person operates. Again, however, there are limitations on the form that the transformation of measurement scales can take. Minimally, the transformation has to leave the dimension of behaviour variables unchanged.

The two postulates make it possible, therefore, to construct dimensionally valid relationships, but they leave the functional form incompletely specified. We still need a third auxiliary postulate.

Let us consider the set of variables that measure the state of a

[1] Luce's analysis (1959) would appear to imply that this constraint arises whenever a relationship is formulated between variables measured on a ratio scale. An alternative hypothesis, which has been suggested by R. Solem, is that physical variables such as mass, distance, and time cannot be allowed to take negative values.

behaviour system at any given time. Within the network of relationships between variables, some variables will be linked directly to one another while others will be linked via intervening variables. In this case, the functional relationship between variables which are more directly linked to one another will be of the simplest form relative to that of variables which are more distantly linked. The third postulate is based, then, on the possibility of identifying sets of variables which are directly linked to one another.

The way in which behaviour variables are linked to one another can vary from person to person. We therefore need to begin by determining for each person the way in which his behaviour variables are linked to one another. Here it is found that the first postulate already provides the basis for a systematic method of determining the location of variables within a network of behaviour variables.

DEFINITIONS

The basic postulates and the derived behaviour principles are restricted to simple behaviour systems. A simple behaviour system is a boundary-maintaining, intrinsically controlled behaviour unit, which, in terms of its operational characteristics, is internally unsegmented into sub-units and externally has no overlap with other behaviour units.

The variables that define the state of a behaviour system are of two types:

(a) The set of variables that specify the internal functioning of the behaviour unit together with all variables that are completely specifiable in terms of internal variables.

(b) The set of variables that specify the transactional relationships between the behavioural unit and its environment. Transactional variables are defined in terms of the internal state of the unit and the simultaneous state of the external environment.

A simple behaviour system can now be defined as a behaviour unit whose state at any given time with respect to any internal or transactional variable is completely specifiable by a *single* measure for each variable.

Thus, if the variables we are concerned with are, say, output rate, work rate, and performance satisfaction, then, in the case of a simple behaviour system, a single measurement scale for each of these variables has to be sufficient to measure at any given time the output rate, the work rate, and the degree of performance satisfaction, and the same has to apply to any other variable in terms of which the state and functioning of a person or group can be described.

Work groups coordinated by a leader, and also experimental situations, are as a rule complex organizations which consist of two systems coupled to one another. Intrinsically controlled autonomous work groups, in which no member takes on a specialist work or leadership role, can operate as a simple behaviour system.

At the level of the individual, a person is a complex behavioural organization, in so far as his activities—in the family, in his job, and in the different organizations to which he may belong—each operate as a boundary-maintaining system. However, any one of these situations may constitute a simple behaviour system.

In each case a necessary condition for the existence of a simple behaviour system is that the operation of the system is based on a task which permits the formulation of a single output measure in terms of which the person or group can measure its performance level.

FIRST POSTULATE

Given a simple behaviour system, then:

Postulate 1

(a) *All variables that refer to the internal state of the system can be defined in terms of the dimension [P].*
(b) *All variables that refer to the transactional state of the system can be defined in terms of the dimension [S].*

Since there are just two basic dimensions apart from time, all functional relationships can be expressed in or reduced to the form $y = f(x, z)$; that is, the value of any behaviour variable is a function of not less than two other behaviour variables, and not more than two other variables are required.[1]

Let us choose as basic variables one variable P from the set of internal variables and a variable S from the set of transactional variables. Given any set of behaviour variables A, B, C ... where

  (a) all measures are representative of the same total behaviour unit,
  (b) all measures refer to the same unit period, and
  (c) parametric steady-state conditions are maintained,

then each behaviour variable can be expressed in terms of the basic variables by means of a functional relationship of the form

$$A = f_1(S,P)$$
$$B = f_2(S,P)$$
$$C = f_3(S,P) \text{ etc.}$$

and, by substitution, each variable can be expressed as a function of any two other variables in the set.

Suppose we start off with four behaviour variables, A, B, C, D. We can in this case formulate two basic equations, say

$$A = f_1(C,D)$$
$$B = f_2(C,D)$$

and from these we can derive all the remaining relationships between these four variables, which are

$$C = f_3(A,B)$$
$$D = f_4(A,B)$$

---

[1] An alternative and more general demonstration will be discussed in a companion volume on socia-technical theory and design. Every law relating behavioural or physical variables can be reduced to or transformed into operational statements which specify an operation π performed on the state of a system S_1, leading to a state of a system S_2:

$$\pi(S_1) \rightarrow S_2$$

In so far as each element corresponds to a variable, the corresponding functional relationship will consist of three variables.

Quite generally, in order to formulate the relation between n variables, we need n-2 functional relationships from which the total set of C_3^n relationships is then derivable. *Table 2* shows, for a given number of variables, how many basic principles have to be formulated, and the number of principles that can be derived.

TABLE 2 THE NUMBER OF BASIC AND DERIVABLE PRINCIPLES FOR A SET OF BEHAVIOUR VARIABLES

Number of variables	Number of basic principles	Number of derivable principles
3	1	0
4	2	2
5	3	7
6	4	16
7	5	30
8	6	50
9	7	113

In theory, any set of principles could be chosen as basic and the remainder as derived principles. This position has often been adopted in mathematical and physical theory construction. In the present case, however, a possible criterion for identifying preferential sets of basic principles exists.

According to the postulate, each variable can be expressed as a function of two other variables. From this it follows that

the functional network for any set of variables of a simple behaviour system is always convertible into a cyclic form.

This is the case since the cyclic network is the only one where each variable always has two neighbours. Let us take as an example a set of five variables, A, B, C, D, E. We can then, if we wish, take any set of three-variable relationships as our basic equations. Suppose we choose

$$A = f_1(B,C)$$

$$B = f_2(E,D)$$

$$C = f_3(B,E)$$

27

which are sufficient to derive the total set of seven equations. These three equations correspond to the network of variables in *Figure 2(a)*.

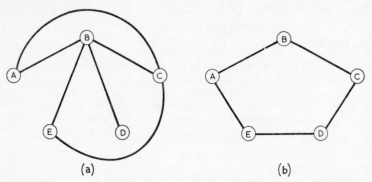

(a)   (b)

FIGURE 2   CONVERSION OF A NETWORK OF RELATIONSHIPS
INTO ITS CYCLIC FORM

The network in this form looks quite complex. However, suppose we write our set of equations instead in the form

$$B = f_1(A,C)$$
$$C = f_2(B,D)$$
$$E = f_3(A,D)$$

then the relationship between the variables will take on the simple form of a cyclic network (*Figure 2(b)*).

Thus by a change in the form of representation a complex network can be converted into a simple cyclic structure.

The simplest set of functional relationships will be that which is based on sets of directly linked variables. In the case of networks of linear or at least approximately monotonic relationships, use can be made of correlation analysis to determine the location of variables within the network.

SECOND POSTULATE

One of the basic sources of differences between persons is the fact that each person operates on the basis of his own measurement scales in terms of which he perceives, evaluates, and responds to events. Now every such measurement scale can be expressed as a transformation of a set of events. If we represent a variable by a set of points on a line, then a given measurement scale can be expressed as a transformation applied to this set of points. The purpose of the second postulate is to define the possible types of measurement scale that may be used. The type of measurement scale according to which the person operates determines the type of metric structure of his behavioural universe. By delimiting the possible types of transformation that measurement scales undergo, we thus delimit the possible types of behavioural universe that can emerge in terms of the possible metric structures on the basis of which they can operate.

Postulate 2

(a) *All internal variables of dimension [P] are subject to linear scale-transformations.*

(b) *All transactional variables of dimension [S] are subject to projective scale-transformations.*

Examples of internal variables of dimension [P] in the case of task performance are work rate, skill level, emotional involvement, boredom, and interest.

Under conditions of outcome predictability, where the performance level is completely determined by the person's work rate and skill level, the performance level or output rate is also an internal variable.

A variable with the dimension $[P^2]$ is performance satisfaction under conditions of outcome predictability. Performance satisfaction is in this case a function both of the performance level and of the performance level relative to the work rate employed.

Let us take as an example a factory worker who bases his measure of performance level P on the quantity of a product X produced over successive unit periods, or a research worker who measures his performance level in terms of the number of papers he publishes. The linear scale-transformation can be put in the form

$$P = \alpha(X - X_0)$$

29

Changes in the value of the parameter α can expand, contract, or reverse the scale values.

If $\alpha = 0$, there will be no relationship between product amount X and the person's performance-level scale. This means that he pursues some other aim in terms of which his performance scale is defined. If α has a negative value, X corresponds to an outcome which is experienced as disadvantageous or harmful.

The measurement problem is that of identifying the outcome criterion X, and ensuring that the transformation parameters maintain steady-state values over the period during which the system is studied.

The value of $\alpha > 0$ gives the rate at which an increase in the product is experienced as an increase in performance level, and X_0, which is the operative zero value of the scale, corresponds to the minimum boundary value below which the performance level cannot go as long as the system operates to maintain its survival conditions.

In a network of functional relationships between behaviour variables the α parameter will combine multiplicatively with other system parameters and may therefore be difficult to estimate quantitatively. The zero points of linear scales, however, remain unaffected, so that simultaneous independent estimates of the location of the zero points are possible. This provides one of the criteria by which the validity of a specific network model can be tested.

While internal variables may be looked at as representations by the system of ongoing internal events, transaction variables imply a representation of external events. The representation obtained depends both on the nature of the external event and on the internal structure of the system. For instance, the degree of stress experienced by a person depends on the aim direction of behaviour and also on the simultaneous incidence of external events which are perceived as blocking or disrupting the conditions for aim achievement. A change in the stress experienced can therefore result either from a change in aim direction or from a change in external events. Thus a scale which, for a given person, functions as a measure of stress, simultaneously defines also his aim, and this in turn defines the scale in terms of which he measures his performance.

According to the second postulate, the personal scales in terms of which transactional variables are measured are related to external scales by a projective transformation. The nature of this kind of transformation is shown in *Figure 3*. $X_1, X_2 \ldots$ represent scale points on the external scale, and 0 the locus of the person. If any additional line is now drawn, then the points of intersection define the position of the corresponding values $S_1, S_2 \ldots$ on the personal scale.

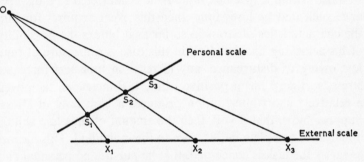

FIGURE 3 THE PROJECTIVE TRANSFORMATION OF AN EXTERNAL MEASUREMENT SCALE INTO A PERSONAL RESPONSE SCALE

The projective transformation is given by the relationship

$$S = \frac{cX+d}{eX+f} \qquad \ldots\ldots(2a)$$

which can be put in the form

$$S = \beta \, \frac{X-X_0}{X-X_\infty} \qquad \ldots\ldots(2b)$$

X_0 in this case corresponds to the zero point of the scale. At X_∞ infinity is reached and the scale values switch from positive to negative values or vice versa. The main characteristic of projective transformations is that, as X increases, the values on the personal scale approach a constant value. The limiting value approached as X increases is β and the rate at which this value is approached depends on the ratio $\dfrac{X_0}{X_\infty}$.

There is one special case where a projective transformation is reduced to a linear one, namely if $e = 0$, and in this case the transformation can be put in the form

$$S = \beta(X - X_0)$$

Let us consider this simplified case to investigate the effect of changes in the value of transformation parameters. We may take as an example a person at work on a task which he wants to finish within a specified time. If he is subjected to a disturbance such that he loses time, then this event acquires for him the characteristics of stress in so far as it blocks the possibility of his achieving his aim. If X in this case is a measure of time lost owing to disturbance, any increase in time lost increases stress, so that β has a positive value. If β increases, then even a relatively short interruption produces a high level of stress. Suppose, now, that $\beta = 0$, then the amount of time lost will be a matter of complete indifference to the individual. This means, as far as the task is concerned, that he pursues no personal aim at all, or that his aim is of a different kind, in which case the type of event that will produce stress, and thus also the appropriate measurement scale, will be different.

Now suppose β is negative, then the scale reverses. The scale in this case does not measure stress, but the opposite. An example would be a situation where a person is forced to carry out a task. In this instance a disturbance that provides an opportunity for stopping work for a while may not be an undesirable event. The same event may thus be experienced as a greater or lesser degree of stress by one person, as no stress by a second, and as an aim-supporting event by a third. Hence no event possesses intrinsic properties of stress. Since the same applies to all transformation scales with respect to α and β parameters, it follows that no event has intrinsic properties either as stress or as an output, no event is intrinsically either pleasant or unpleasant, attractive or repulsive, rewarding or punishing, but an event can acquire these characteristics with respect to a survival-maintaining transformation network and depending on the metric of the operative transformation processes.

Since projective scale-transformations leave none of the metric properties of a scale unchanged, the question arises whether there is any scale characteristic that remains invariant. It is shown in projective geometry that there is one measure that does remain invariant: it is given by the cross ratio between points $X_1 X_2 X_3 X_4$, defined by the expression

$$\frac{(X_1 - X_2)(X_3 - X_4)}{(X_2 - X_3)(X_4 - X_1)}$$

Whatever linear or projective transformation is applied to the scale values, the cross ratio will always retain the same value. What is interesting about the cross ratio is that it is definable without having to specify a measure of distance between points. All that is required for the type of construction shown in *Figure 3* is an axiom of points and the incidence of points on a line, where a line is defined in terms of any two points. (Dually we can start off with an axiom of a line and define points in terms of intersection of lines.) This means that it should be possible to formulate behaviour theory in terms of non-metrical projective geometry and its associated algebra.

METHODOLOGICAL IMPLICATIONS

The two postulates provide the basis for theory construction, and provide at the same time the necessary methodological conditions, all of which have to be satisfied for testing behaviour principles. These may be summarized as follows:

1a. In order to satisfy the characteristics of a simple behaviour system, the behaviour unit has to be chosen so that each variable can be completely specified by a single measure.

1b. All measures have to refer to the same total behaviour unit.

2a. The unit period of observation has to be chosen so that the

33

state of the system can be completely specified by a single measure.

2b. All measures have either to be simultaneous or to refer to the same total unit period.

3. All measures have to be formulated in terms of the same frame of reference, and this should be the set of measurement scales on the basis of which the person or group studied itself operates.

4. The measurement technique has to provide for the simultaneous measurement of at least three, and preferably more than three, variables. The larger the number of variables that can be measured, the more extensive and rigorous the tests that can be made of any one hypothesis that may be formulated.

5. All parameters of the behaviour unit must have reached, and must maintain, parametric steady-state conditions during the recording period.

CHAPTER 4

Cyclic Network Analysis

————◆————

SUMMARY

If the relationships between behaviour variables are linear or at least monotonic, then a simple technique based on partial correlation analysis makes it possible to map out the network of relationships and to determine the location of each variable in the network.

Analysis of data from the pupil-task study led to the discovery that both the network of relationships and the direction of relationships between variables can differ from case to case.

A formal analysis of network properties shows that there exist intrinsic constraints which make it possible for only a limited number of network structures to exist.

————◆————

ONE OF the consequences of the first postulate has been shown to be that the network of relationships between variables of a simple behaviour system is convertible into a cyclic form.

We shall in the following restrict ourselves to the simplest case where the network is composed of linear or monotonic relationships. Suppose that the correct cyclic order for a set of variables is that shown in *Figure 4*. The link between adjoining variables is either $+1$ (positive) or -1 (negative).

Now consider the effect of an increase in the value of A on B. If E is held constant then the effect must travel via D. The product of the signs *en route* is $(+1)(+1) = +1$, so that, with E constant, an increase in A increases B.

Suppose, now, that D is held constant, then the effect must travel via E and C. The product of the signs *en route* is $(-1)(+1)(+1) = -1$, so that, with D constant, an increase in A decreases B.

35

In this case, the partial correlation of A with B should be positive with E or C held constant and negative with D constant. A hypothetical network is confirmed if

(i)   the direction of the predicted relationship between every pair of variables, keeping each of the intervening variables constant, is the same as the direction of the corresponding partial correlation, and if

(ii) for every pair of variables which are directly linked neighbours, the partial correlations do not change sign when any other variable is held constant.

Having identified the location of variables in the above network we can then go on to formulate three basic functional equations, choosing sets of variables which are immediate neighbours, and test these by the fit obtained for the seven derived functional relationships.

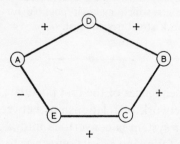

FIGURE 4 ILLUSTRATIVE CYCLIC NETWORK COMPOSED OF LINEAR OR MONOTONIC RELATIONSHIPS

Table 3 shows the partial correlation results obtained in the autonomous group study for the relationship between output rate, work rate of team members, level of integration defined in terms of the effectiveness with which group activities are co-ordinated, and amount of stress defined in terms of events which hinder and disrupt the work of the group directed to the achievement of its performance aim.

In order to construct the network of variables shown in *Figure 5*, we need to determine first the location of variables in the network. This is most easily done by noting the pairs of variables whose partial correlations change sign depending on which other variable is kept constant. These pairs of variables are therefore not direct neighbours.

It is found in this case that stress and output rate are not directly linked and that work rate and level of integration are

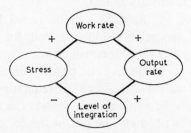

FIGURE 5 NETWORK OF BEHAVIOUR PRINCIPLES FOUND IN THE STUDY OF AUTONOMOUS WORK GROUPS

TABLE 3 PARTIAL CORRELATION TEST OF THE BEHAVIOUR NETWORK SHOWN IN FIGURE 5

Relationship between:	Kept constant	Predicted direction of the relationship	$r_{xy.z}$
Output rate, Work rate	Integration	+	+ ·90
	Stress	+	+ ·95
Output rate, Integration	Work rate	+	+ ·91
	Stress	+	+ ·86
Stress, Output rate	Integration	+	+ ·59
	Work rate	−	− ·89
Stress, Work rate	Integration	+	+ ·86
	Output rate	+	+ ·95
Stress, Integration	Output rate	−	− ·64
	Work rate	−	− ·73
Work rate, Integration	Stress	+	+ ·71
	Output rate	−	− ·78

not directly linked. All the remaining pairs of variables must be directly linked and this is confirmed by the fact that their partial correlations do not change sign. The directional sign for each link, that is whether it is positive or negative, is then given by the directional sign of the partial correlation for each pair of variables that is directly linked.

The validity of the network can be tested by comparing the direction of the relationship obtained for each pair of variables, keeping one variable constant, with the corresponding partial correlation obtained. Four partial correlations are required to specify the network. The eight remaining relationships are derivable from the network and provide the validity test.

The network obtained can be put in the form of two basic principles:

1. Output rate directly increases with work rate and level of integration.
2. Stress directly increases the work rate and/or decreases the level of integration.

The two derivable principles, which concern the effect of stress on output, are:

    I. Stress increases the output rate if the level of integration remains constant.
   II. Stress decreases the output rate if the work rate remains constant.

The next step is to construct the functional relationships for the set of basic principles, based on variables which are directly linked to one another. From these the total network of functional relationships becomes derivable. This is carried out in Chapter 6.

We now turn to another study which shows that neither the linkage between behaviour variables nor the direction of the relationships is necessarily universal. There may in the first example be inherent task constraints which restrict the possible behaviour networks that can emerge. This will in fact be shown to be the case. However, if as in the following example there exist no inherent constraints deriving from the task structure, then there appear to be no *a priori* constraints either on the location of behaviour variables in the network or on the direction of the relationship between behaviour variables.

The data are from the cross-sectional technique applied to the study of the pupil and his task at school. The situation in this case is one of outcome uncertainty since there is no necessary relationship between work effort and skill level during the course of study, and the final grade obtained on the basis of an examination.

Figure 6 shows the networks of near-monotonic relationships obtained for two girls, which can, to begin with, be obtained directly by inspection of three-variable data plots. The cyclic networks are composed of two sets of relationships.

In the case of Elly:

1.   Work effort increases with work effort judged to be required and/or increases with the degree of anxiety.
2.   Boredom increases with work effort judged to be required and/or decreases with the degree of anxiety.

In the case of Berit:

1.   Work effort increases with work effort judged to be required and/or decreases with the degree of boredom experienced.
2.   Boredom decreases with the degree of work effort and/or increases with the degree of anxiety.

Table 4 shows the direction, obtained from the network, of the twelve relationships between every pair of variables, keeping one other variable constant, and the values obtained by partial correlations from the data. Four relationships of this type are required to specify the model. The directions of the remaining eight partial correlations are all in agreement with the model.

From *Table 4* the network structure can now be written down straight away by noting that, in the case of Elly, a direct link does not exist between boredom and work effort or between work effort required and anxiety, since the direction of the relationship depends on which intervening variable is kept constant. The direction of the remaining pairs of adjoining variables is given by the direction of the partial correlations.

The relationships between behaviour variables will be seen to be fundamentally different for these two individuals.

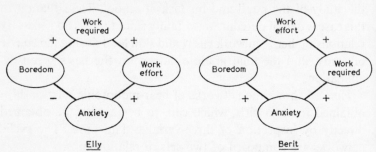

Elly   Berit

FIGURE 6 TWO DIFFERENT NETWORKS OF BEHAVIOUR PRINCIPLES FOUND IN THE STUDY OF PUPIL-TASK RELATIONSHIPS AT SCHOOL

TABLE 4   PARTIAL CORRELATION TEST OF THE BEHAVIOUR NETWORK SHOWN IN FIGURE 6

Relationship between:	Kept constant	Elly Predicted $r_{xy,z}$		Berit Predicted $r_{xy,z}$	
Work effort, Work required	Boredom	+	+ ·95	+	+ ·80
	Anxiety	+	+ ·79	+	+ ·87
Work effort, Anxiety	Work required	+	+ ·79	−	− ·54
	Boredom	+	+ ·90	+	+ ·69
Boredom, Work required	Work effort	+	+ ·81	+	+ ·15
	Anxiety	+	+ ·87	−	− ·83
Boredom, Work effort	Work required	−	− ·81	−	− ·60
	Anxiety	+	+ ·59	−	− ·82
Anxiety, Work required	Work effort	−	− ·41	+	+ ·83
	Boredom	+	+ ·92	+	+ ·92
Anxiety, Boredom	Work required	−	− ·91	+	+ ·70
	Work effort	−	− ·72	+	+ ·44

In both cases work effort and work effort required are directly linked and boredom and anxiety are directly linked. However, for Elly, boredom and anxiety are negatively linked whereas for Berit they are positively linked. In the case of Elly, anxiety is linked to work effort, whereas for Berit anxiety is linked to the amount of work she perceives is required. Consequently, for Elly, boredom is related to work effort required whereas for Berit it is related to the amount of work carried out.

Elly's work effort increases with the work effort required and anxiety experienced. Berit's work effort also increases with the work effort required but it decreases with the anxiety experienced about examination results.

Elly responds to increased anxiety about examination results by decreased boredom and/or increased work effort. Berit responds to increased anxiety by increased boredom and/or increased work effort.

The conditions under which boredom is experienced are completely reversed. In the case of Elly, boredom increases with work effort required and decreases with anxiety experienced. In the case of Berit, boredom decreases with work effort required and increases with anxiety experienced.

These two cases were by no means chosen to illustrate extreme differences. They are, in fact, more similar to one another than to other cases which have been examined. What they have in common is that a linkage of near-monotonic relationships exists between these four variables.

One rather intriguing result is that all the four-variable networks found so far consist of three positive and one negative link. A study of the properties of linear cyclic networks shows that in fact the possible distributions of signs are quite limited.

PROPERTIES OF LINEAR NETWORKS

The basic properties of linear networks will in the following be discussed by analysing the characteristics of networks consisting of four variables. Most of the results are easily generalizable to larger sets of variables.

The linear network of four variables can be represented by a set of equations:

$$A = \alpha C + \beta D \qquad \text{......(1)}$$

$$B = \gamma C + \delta D \qquad \text{......(2)}$$

$$\alpha, \beta, \gamma, \delta \text{ and } (\alpha\delta - \beta\gamma) \neq 0$$

The two remaining equations that can be derived are:

$$A = \frac{\beta}{\delta} B + \left(\frac{\alpha\delta - \beta\gamma}{\delta}\right) C \qquad \text{......(I)}$$

$$A = \frac{\alpha}{\gamma} B - \left(\frac{\alpha\delta - \beta\gamma}{\gamma}\right) D \qquad \text{......(II)}$$

The additive parameters which will normally appear in linear equations are neglected since they do not affect the direction of relationships.

The expression $(\alpha\delta - \beta\gamma) \neq 0$ will generally be either positive or negative so that we get two sets of derived equations. Moreover, if δ and γ have the same sign then the coefficients of C and D in Equations I and II must be opposite in sign. Most of the basic network properties hinge on these two facts. Since there are four parameters which may have either a positive or a

Possible networks

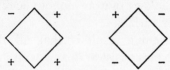

Impossible networks

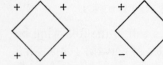

FIGURE 7   POSSIBLE AND IMPOSSIBLE NETWORKS COMPOSED OF FOUR VARIABLES

negative sign, there are $4^2 = 16$ possible sets of basic equations.

To turn now to the networks that can be constructed, there are, in terms of distribution of positive and negative signs, six types of cyclic network. It will be shown that only two of these can exist (*Figure 7*).

Theorem 1. The only four-variable networks that can exist are those that consist of

(a) one positive link, the remainder being negative;
(b) one negative link, the remainder being positive.

Proof: The possible three-variable networks are of the type

$$A = B + C$$

A increases with B and C. With A constant, B decreases with C. In this case two links are positive and one is negative, and

$$A = -B - C$$

which gives a network where all three links are negative.

Let us now introduce a fourth variable D. If D is inserted between two variables which have a positive link, then the products of links via D must be positive, i.e. either $(++)$ or $(--)$.

If the link is negative, then the products of links via D must be $(-+)$.

Figure 8 shows that the only four-variable networks that can be constructed have either one positive link or one negative link.

Theorem 2. If A and B are both affected by C and D in the same way (α and γ have the same sign and β and δ have the same sign), then A and B are immediate neighbours and the link between them is positive.

If A and B are affected in opposite ways by C and D then A and B are immediate neighbours and the link between them is negative.

Proof: If α approaches the value of γ and β approaches the value of δ, then A and B merge with one another and become the same variable. A and B must therefore be immediate neighbours so that their merger can be achieved without affecting the remainder of the network.

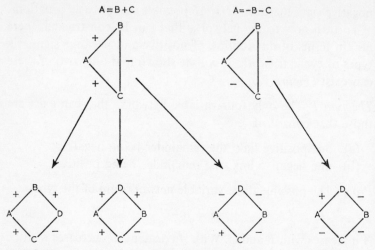

FIGURE 8 TRANSITION POSSIBILITIES FROM THREE-VARIABLE
TO FOUR-VARIABLE NETWORKS

If α and γ have the same sign, and β and δ have the same sign, then both α/γ and β/δ are positive. In this case A increases with B both with C constant and with D constant. The link between A and B is therefore positive.

If α and γ are of opposite sign, and β and δ are of opposite sign, then both α/γ and β/δ are negative. The link between A and B is therefore negative.

We can now apply the two theorems to demonstrate the network properties of the set of linear equations. For the sake of convenience we shall write the equations without the quantitative parameters, thus indicating only whether one variable increases or decreases with another under given conditions.

If all parameters are positive

$$A = C + D$$

$$B = C + D$$

A and B have a similar relation to C and D. A and B are therefore neighbours with a direct link. Both with A and with B constant the relationship between C and D is negative. The link between C and D is therefore negative.

There are two sets of derived equations, depending on whether $(\alpha\delta - \beta\gamma)$ is positive or negative:

either $A = B + C$

$\qquad A = B - D$

or $\qquad A = B - C$

$\qquad A = B + D$

Reversal in the value of $(\alpha\delta - \beta\gamma)$ inverts the location of C and D.
If

$$A = C + D$$

$$B = -C - D$$

then A and B have opposite relations to C and D. The direct link between A and B is therefore negative. The link between C and D is negative. The two sets of derived equations are

$\qquad A = -B + D$

$\qquad A = -B - C$

and $\qquad A = -B - D$

$\qquad A = -B + C$

Reversal in the value of $(\alpha\delta - \beta\gamma)$ in this case reverses the location of the opposite $+$, $-$ signs.
If

$$A = C - D$$

$$B = -C + D$$

then the link between A and B is negative and the link between C and D is positive.

45

The two sets of derived equations are

$$A = -B + C$$
$$A = -B + D$$

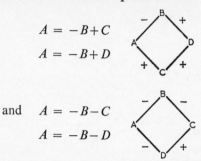

and
$$A = -B - C$$
$$A = -B - D$$

Reversal in the value of $(\alpha\delta - \beta\gamma)$ reverses both the location of C and D, and the direction of the opposite $+$ signs.

Finally, if

$$A = C - D$$
$$B = C + D$$

A and B are not neighbours; $(\alpha\delta - \beta\gamma)$ must have a positive value. There is in this case only one possible set of derived equations

$$A = -B + C$$
$$A = B - D$$

The largest network of linear and monotonic relationships discovered so far consists of five variables. There is, however, no difficulty in extending the analysis theoretically to larger sets of variables.

Using the method employed in proving Theorem 2, we find

Number of variables	Possible number of positive links
3	0, 2
4	1, 3
5	0, 2, 4
6	1, 3, 5

and we arrive inductively at:

Theorem 3. In an n-variable linear network, the possible number of positive links is given by the series

$$n-1, n-3, n-5 \ldots \geqslant 0$$

CHAPTER 5

Basic Concepts in the Study of Behaviour Systems and the Nature of Behavioural Laws

———◆———

SUMMARY

The statement 'I act' may be separated into the 'I' that acts and the 'activity'. If we follow this usage we arrive at the Lewinian life-space concept of a person and his psychological environment, which consists of potential activities. The person is looked at as a system of tension regions which are related to the positive and negative valences of corresponding activities.

Here it is possible to be misled by the theory on which our conventional language is based. We say 'the table has legs' and thus assert that there exists a table apart from the board and legs. However, there is no table apart from the board and legs. The legs form part of the table. We say 'the lightning flashes' but the lightning and the flash are one and the same thing.

If we represent the person in terms of the activities he engages in, that is, we say the activities form part of the person, we arrive at the behaviour system concept. Motivation and emotions can then no longer be considered as belonging to a separate system which is linked to behaviour, but have to be looked at as characteristics of a behaviour structure.

The successive stages in the reformulation of the Lewinian life-space concept are reported in Herbst, 1949, 1951, 1954a, 1957a. The following chapter summarizes the basic concepts required for the conceptual representation of behaviour systems. A more detailed presentation can be found in Herbst, 1961, 1962.

———◆———

THE TERM *behaviour system* is used to refer to the representation of both individuals and groups in terms of their activities.

The term *system* is used to refer to a set of activity elements which

(i) are interdependent with respect to their functioning and
(ii) operate as a boundary-maintaining unit.

An *activity* is defined in terms of an initial or input state S_1, which is submitted to a sequence of operations π, leading to a final or output state S_2

$$\pi(S_1) \to S_2$$

If, for a given initial state and operations, the same final state always results, then the task is said to be determinate and a situation of *outcome predictability* is said to exist. If the outcome is not predictable then the task is indeterminate and a situation of *outcome uncertainty* is said to exist.

The *action level* of a behaviour system is defined in terms of

(i) the number of active components of the system
(ii) the rate of functioning of components and
(iii) the *level of integration*, that is the effectiveness with which the functioning of individual components is interwoven, coordinated, and combined into a functioning unit.

In the study of groups, we may take either group activities or group members as components of the system. If we adopt the latter form of representation, then the action level of the group is definable in terms of

(i) the number of active group members
(ii) the work rate of group members
(iii) the level of group integration defined in terms of the interrelationship maintained between individuals in on-going group activities.

The constituents of the action level may be taken as the axes of an action space.

A necessary condition for system survival is that the action level is maintained within a bounded region of the action space. The *operational boundary* of the system includes minimum boundary values for the number of components, the activity rate, and the level of integration.

To the extent that behaviour becomes aim-oriented, and a state of *task involvement* exists, regions within the action space acquire the characteristics of *strain* (experienced as unpleasure and distress) and *balance* (experienced as pleasure and ease). Conditions of strain and balance can be represented as a deformation of the action space. The greater the degree of task involvement given by the degree of distortion of the action space, the greater the potential degree of strain and balance within the system.

Conditions of strain and balance lead to a process to maintain specific sets of activities, specific activity rates, and a specific interrelationship of activity components, and to exclude others, thus creating and maintaining a *functional boundary* of the system. At the same time, the system now operates so as to achieve and maintain a specific action level which defines the *output* of the system. The maintenance of system survival not only demands that the output achieved satisfies the operative aim of the system. System survival requires also that a stable link is maintained to external units, which can utilize the output in exchange for *inputs* that the system requires to maintain its functioning. The input-transformation-output-conversion-input process, which involves both the system and one or more external supporting units, is referred to as a *positive dependence cycle*.

In so far as behaviour is aim-directed, external events acquire the characteristic of aim support or aim interference. *Stress* constitutes a negative input for the system, which interferes with or disrupts any part of the positive dependence cycle on which system-functioning is based.

Stress counteraction may be separated into three successive phases:

1. *External adjustment processes,* concerned with neutralizing or sealing off the stress-inducing agent in order to maintain or re-establish the boundary conditions of the system.

2. *Dislocation control*, concerned with repairing and making good any damage that has occurred in the course of stress incidence in order to re-establish the internal, and if necessary also the external, process structure of the system.

3. *Interference control*, which comes into operation when the system again switches back to its normal aimed-for mode of functioning, and is concerned with compensating as far as possible for the loss of time and effort diverted to the preceding stress-counteraction phases.

The coming into operation of any one of the above stress-counteraction phases provides behavioural evidence for a state of stress of the system. Further, identification of the types of event that produce a state of stress makes it possible to infer the operative aim of the system.

Maintenance of a system boundary implies the maintenance of some degree of stress. This is the case since the system boundary comes into existence as a result of processes to achieve and maintain specific activity components and structures and to eject and avoid others. The deployment of effort to keep some event states outside the system and maintain others inside implies in either case an opposition between internal and external processes.

To the extent that the degree of stress goes below or rises above an optimal stress level, a condition of strain arises. If the system operates to maintain the degree of strain within an acceptable range, then the system boundary will be maintained homeostatically.

If stress is too low, strain may manifest itself in the form of boredom or of dislike of the situation, or in the form of fear and anxiety in response to the potential threat of system dissolution. Processes will in this case come into operation to create opposition with the environment, so as to increase the strength of the system boundaries.

If stress becomes excessive, the system faces the potential threat of destruction, and stress-counteraction processes will come into operation which, to the extent that they are successful, will reduce the degree of stress.

The functioning of behaviour systems is subject to three performance-evaluation mechanisms, all of which are based on the output that the system operates so as to achieve:

1. The output achieved relative to the cost and effort invested determines *performance satisfaction*.
2. The output achieved relative to reciprocated input received determines *input satisfaction*.
3. The output achieved relative to the degree of task involvement determines the degree of *strain* and *balance* manifested in the form of dislike and liking of the situation respectively. Strain increases both when the output level maintained by the system becomes too low relative to task involvement (hyper-cathexis) and when it becomes relatively too high (hypo-cathexis).

It follows that system-functioning cannot be goal-directed in any simple kind of way since an attempt to maximize with respect to any one performance-evaluation criterion will result in sub-optimization with respect to other performance criteria.

It is important to distinguish between two fundamentally different conditions under which a variable may have a zero value. If y is dependent on x and z, and the relationship is

$$y = \alpha xz$$

then y will become temporarily zero whenever x or z becomes zero. However, if the parameter α is zero, then y will be zero for any values of x and z. In this case, if the *linkage parameter* α becomes zero, all three variables will become *inoperative*.

Thus, if emotional involvement exists, then, dependent on the concomitant degree of strain and balance, the situation may be experienced as liked, disliked, or ambivalent. If there is temporarily no involvement, then indifference is experienced. However, if involvement becomes inoperative, neither liking nor dislike can come into operation under any conditions and a state of equanimity with respect to events results.

51

A behaviour system constitutes a network of mutually dependent system characteristics in which no one set of variables can be picked out as being logically or causally prior.

No event has intrinsic characteristics of stress, strain, output, etc., but events acquire these characteristics in so far as a behaviour structure of mutually dependent elements is evolved which operates so as to maintain its survival. To the extent that behaviour is aim-directed, events acquire the characteristic of being aim-supporting or -opposing, of being valuable and desirable or repugnant and undesirable, of constituting achievement or failure. The structure created in turn provides the condition whereby aim-directed behaviour is generated to cope with distress, to counteract stress, or to maintain the condition for pleasant and desirable states.

The mode of functioning of the system depends on the specific type of linkage established between behaviour variables and on its linkage parameters.

A behaviour system will cease to function if its organizational structure is dissolved or destroyed, the system boundaries no longer operate, and no output is produced which is needed to maintain the essential transactional process with the environment. This means that variables such as output, work rate, integration level all have a zero value. This, however, is not necessarily the end of the system since the fact that activity variables of the system have a zero value does not affect the parametric linkage structure of relationships between behaviour variables.

To the extent that emotional involvement exists but achievement-oriented behaviour is no longer possible, a state of strain and distress will be maintained so that, under suitable conditions, the re-emergence and building up of a new phase of the system will provide a route for strain reduction.

The fact that a system has ceased to function does not, therefore, imply that it has ceased to exist. The existence of a behaviour system is based on its potential for imposing on events a particular type of structure that it seeks to achieve and maintain. The structure imposed is given by the linkage network of behaviour variables, which determines the way in which events are experienced and responded to.

A behaviour system will cease to operate only when the dependence linkages between behaviour variables are broken, which occurs when the linkage parameters take on a zero value. Whereas, before, only the variables of system-functioning took on a zero value, now, with the structural parameters inoperative, all system characteristics become inoperative.

With the cessation of a behaviour system nothing goes out of existence. The term inoperative has been used to indicate that events which have acquired specific characteristics within a functioning system structure—such as of stress, of aim achievement, of fear and anxiety, of being desirable or repulsive—no longer have these characteristics and are thus no longer experienced and responded to in this way.

THE NATURE OF BEHAVIOURAL LAWS

The basic difference between non-living matter and living beings is that the former is subject to laws whereas the latter create the laws that determine their behaviour. Every person as a result of his aim-directed behaviour builds a behavioural universe and the laws in terms of which it operates. Each motivated action in the present reconstitutes the existing structure or, going beyond the boundary of the existing phase of the system, leads to developmental structural change. We cannot assume that in the course of developmental changes the succeeding phase will necessarily be superior to the previous phase. Both evolution and involution are possible developmental paths. We do not as yet have a theory which makes it possible to predict the effect of actions on the future structural state of a behaviour system.

If at some time in the future it becomes possible to formulate the developmental laws of behaviour, we will be in a position to derive and formulate what are essentially moral and ethical laws in terms of the types of action that predictably lead to evolutionary and involutionary developmental changes.

Involutionary changes are definable as those whereby behaviour becomes increasingly blindly mechanical and less subject to self-control, the transformation of phenomena to which the system responds is rigid and distorted by the existing behaviour structure, and the range of conditions under which suffering is experienced is increased. Evolutionary changes, on the other hand, are those that lead to the development of behaviour organizations which are less rigidly bound by quasi-mechanical laws, have increased self-control, produce less transformational distortion of phenomena, and are less likely to engage in actions that result in suffering for themselves and others. In so far as the behavioural universe is built up as a result of past actions, and present actions in turn contribute to its future structure, every person is at least in a causal sense fully responsible for his actions. He cannot escape the effect of his actions which, having been done, become a part of the existing structure of his behavioural universe and condition its future development. The moral laws are likely to have an invariant form, applicable to every behavioural universe whatever its existing structure. Unlike structural laws, which under parametric steady-state conditions take on a deterministic form, developmental laws will require the use of stochastic models.

If the network of behavioural laws is self-created, there must also be conditions where these laws, in any of the forms they may take, cease to operate. The laws of behaviour, whatever their ultimate form, come into operation whenever behaviour is aim-directed in terms of desire and aversion. Under these conditions, events acquire the characteristic of supporting or opposing, of aim achievement or of failure; they acquire finite measurable characteristics and become interlocked in structures which can operate and maintain themselves in a quasi-mechanical way. This is one mode, but not the only one, of experiencing and responding to the world. If no directional structure is imposed by wanting and not wanting, the same events, deprived of the coordinate scheme in terms of which they are apprehended, cease to be measurable, and behavioural laws cease to operate.

Each behavioural universe represents a network of transformation processes, and, dependent on the transformation
process, events acquire the characteristic of being desirable or
undesirable, of supporting or opposing. Each behavioural
universe is thus a subjective world. There are, then, a multitude
of behavioural universes, each of which is a subjective world,
and there is a non-subjective world in which events, being
untransformed, exist as intrinsically neither desirable nor undesirable, neither opposing nor supporting. This non-subjective
world is coextensive with the totality of behavioural universes
each of which distorts and refracts events in terms of its
individual process structure. It is a curious paradox that it is
only within each of these subjective transformation systems
that behavioural laws can apply. The non-subjective world,
in which the same events are untransformed and undistorted,
lies beyond the boundaries of science. It is not measurable nor
can it be conceptualized, since measurement and conceptualization imply a transformation process operating within one or
other behavioural universe.

PART TWO

Principles of Behaviour

CHAPTER 6

Principles of Behaviour under Conditions of Outcome Predictability

The Longitudinal Parametric Steady-state Technique

————◆————

SUMMARY

The longitudinal case-study technique can be applied to persons or groups working on a repetitive task. Measures are obtained for successive task-cycle units which can be used to determine the network of relationships between behaviour variables for each individual case.

A network of behaviour principles found in the study of an autonomous work group is shown to be theoretically derivable from the basic postulates. Further, the possible types of task structure, each of which provides the basis for a different range of behavioural universes that can evolve, are found to be derivable. The results obtained suggest a basis for a quantitative theory of socio-technical organization.

————◆————

THE BASIC model of the longitudinal case-study technique is as follows. Given a person or group with a repetitive task-cycle unit, which can be measured in terms of a set of variables $x, y, z \ldots$ all of which are representative of the same total task unit, and representative of the total cycle unit, a set of measures $(x_1, y_1, z_1 \ldots), (x_2, y_2, z_2 \ldots)$ for successive cycle units is obtained. Provided parametric steady-state conditions are maintained, the sequence of cycle units can be disregarded. The measures in this case constitute different possible states of the same system, and three-variable data plots can be used to determine the network of relationships between system variables.

The necessary methodological conditions for this technique, which are based on the theoretical requirements obtained from the basic postulates (Chapter 3), are:

(i) The behaviour unit chosen for study has to satisfy the characteristics of a simple behaviour system so that its state at any given time with respect to any internal or transactional variable is completely specifiable by a single measure for each variable.

(ii) The existence of sufficiently identical task-cycles, which can be used as units of analysis. Specifically, the structural characteristics of the task and the operative aim should remain unchanged throughout the recording period.

(iii) Systematic, continuous, behaviour-recording to obtain data on as many cycle units as possible.

(iv) The formulation of measures all of which are representative of the same total behaviour cycle.

(v) A steady state of system parameters during the recording period. This means in practice that periods of learning, reorganization, and restructuring, in so far as these involve a change in system parameters, will need to be separately considered.

(vi) Ideally, all variables should be free to vary over the largest possible range of values, subject only to the requirement that critical limits, beyond which changes in the value of parameters are induced, should not be exceeded.

(vii) The recording technique should be one that provides measures for the widest possible range of variables of system-functioning. This is essential in order to make it possible to test the validity of each measurement scale for the specific system studied. At the same time, the larger the number of variables measured, the more rigorous and extensive the tests that can be made of the consistency of any one hypothesis that may be formulated.

This method was applied to the study of a seven-man composite autonomous work team in a British coalmine (Herbst, 1962). In this type of work organization the group takes over complete responsibility for the total cycle of operations involved in mining at the coalface. No member of the group has a fixed work role. Instead, the men deploy themselves in accordance with the requirements of the ongoing group task. Within the limits of technological and safety requirements, they are free to evolve their own way of organizing and carrying out their task. They are not subject to any external authority in this respect, nor is there within the group itself any member who takes over a formal directive leadership function. Whereas, in the conventional work organization, the task is split into four to eight separate work roles carried out by different men and paid for at different rates, in the composite group, members are no longer paid for the type of work carried out. Payment was based instead on a contract negotiated between the team delegate and management, which included an agreement on the price per ton of coal produced by the team. The income obtained was divided equally among the team members. The formation of the team was based on self-selection, which is a traditional technique in the coalfield where the study took place.

The conditions under which the group worked provided in some respects an almost ideal natural research laboratory. Since all the men participated in production work, and control and coordination of work activities were carried out by the group itself, the criteria for a simple behaviour system were satisfied. In the absence of a formal work routine, group functioning could respond freely to changing conditions, within the limits of existing task constraints. Lack of a formal and enforceable work routine provided at the same time a condition in which detailed work data, which normally might be difficult to obtain or liable to distortion, had the nature of neutral information, and became more easily available.

Measures were obtained by means of a continuous work record maintained by the team, which made it possible to determine, for each team member, which of the component activities of the task he was working on, for how long, and with whom. The record was kept for three months, which was the total life-period of the team. The group task consisted of a repetitive work-cycle which took about three to five days to complete. A set of seven measures was obtained for each cycle unit.

It took the group about one and a half weeks of working together before parameters of group functioning were stabilized at steady-state values, so that for the subsequent period a network of functional relationships between variables of group functioning emerged, which could be formulated and tested.

The network of functional relationships was in this case concerned with a condition of *outcome predictability*, which may be defined as a situation where the output rate of the system is predictable as a function of the rate of operation of activity elements which form part of the system and of the degree of integration of activity processes.

Necessary conditions for outcome predictability to exist are:

(i) that the group task is such that from a given initial input state of the system there is a known sequence structure of operations which will predictably lead to a given output state, and

(ii) that the team has full autonomous control over all task-relevant operations.

It will be shown in the following that a network of functional relationships, which it was possible to formulate and test in this study, is derivable as a special case from the postulates of generalized behaviour theory. Specifically it will be shown that, under conditions of outcome predictability, the possible networks of behaviour principles that can come into being are restricted by the structural characteristics of the group task.

The derivation of behaviour principles proceeds in six steps:

(i) Determination of the dimension of behaviour variables which can be either internal variables definable in terms of the dimension $[P]$ or transactional variables definable in terms of the dimension $[S]$.

(ii) Construction of a set of basic dimensional equations. Where possible, use is at this stage made of cyclic network analysis to identify directly linked sets of variables.

(iii) Conversion of the dimensional equations into a functional form.

(iv) Specification of the functional form of the dimensional equations, making use of Postulate 3 (see page 70).

(v) Substitution of the appropriate scale transformations for each variable given by Postulate 2.

(vi) Identification of parameters and derivation of special cases.

We shall be concerned with a set of six variables of group functioning, as shown in *Table 5*. A basic set of four equations of the form $y = f(x, z)$ is in this case required from which the total network of sixteen equations is derivable.

The four basic principles found in the autonomous group study are:

Principle 1. The output rate (P) of the group is an additive function of the work rate of team members (W) and of the level of group integration (G). The level of integration is defined in terms of the effectiveness with which group members cooperate in carrying out the group task.

Principle 2. Stress (S) increases the work rate of team members (W) and/or decreases the level of group integration (G).

Principle 3. Performance satisfaction (F) increases with the output rate achieved (P) and the extent to which the output rate achieved is high relative to the work rate (W) employed.

Principle 6. Stress (S) increases the output rate if task involvement (V) is below a critical value, and decreases the output rate if task involvement is above the critical value.[1]

---

[1] The remaining principles 4 and 5 concern the degree of balance and strain of the system. Neither variable appears in the present case to be directly linked to any of the above pairs of variables.

TABLE 5 VARIABLES OF AUTONOMOUS GROUP FUNCTIONING

Variable	Symbol	Dimension	Behaviour system concept	Measure
Work rate	W	P	Rate of functioning of activity elements of the system which contribute to the output rate	Production rate of the group on a component task where group members work independently of one another
Level of integration	G	P	Effectiveness with which activity processes which contribute to the output rate are coordinated	Based on the rate of change in subgroup structure in carrying out the task (low) and on the transition distance between successive subgroup structures (high)
Output rate (performance level)	P	P	Production rate in terms of the operative achievement aim of the system	Coal tonnage produced per manshift over the total work-cycle, convertible into monetary income values
Stress	S	S	Extent to which external events disrupt or block activity processes which contribute to the output rate	Amount of time lost owing to technical breakdowns
Task involvement	V	P	Extent to which system-functioning is aim-directed; emotional involvement can be conceptualized as a distortion of the action space, producing regions of strain (negative valence) and balance (positive valence)	Number of team members who take the risk, under underground conditions, of working temporarily isolated from other team members in order to facilitate work progress
Performance satisfaction	F	P2	Evaluation of output rate achieved relative to cost in the form of work effort expended	Level of satisfaction with group functioning and performance level achieved

The following basic set of equations was formulated and tested in this study, and will be shown to be derivable from the postulates of generalized behaviour theory.

$$P - P_0 = \left(\frac{W - W_0}{a} \right) + b(G - G_0) \qquad \dots\dots(1)$$

$$W = e(G - G_0) \frac{S + c}{S + d} + W_0 \qquad \dots\dots(2)$$

$$F = g(P - P_0) \left[(P - P_0) - f(W - W_0) \right] \qquad \dots\dots(3)$$

$$P = n \frac{(V - V_c)(S_c - S)}{S + k} + P_c \qquad \dots\dots(6)$$

where P_0 = minimum boundary value of the output rate
W_0 = minimum boundary value of the work rate
G_0 = minimum boundary value of the level of integration.

Restrictions of variables with respect to range are:

$$G \geqslant G_0 > 0 \qquad S, V \geqslant 0$$

Parametric conditions which determine the direction of relationships between variables are:

$$W_0 > 0, \qquad P_c > P_0 > 0, \qquad S_c > 0$$

$$a \geqslant 1, \qquad b,c,d,e,g,n > 0$$

$$k = \frac{ec + abd}{e + ab}$$

$$d > k > c, \qquad f > \frac{1}{a}$$

From the four basic principles the total network of sixteen functional relationships is derivable. The problem of parametric estimation is in this case that of finding a set of parameter values for the set of basic principles which will provide a fit for the total network of basic and derived equations.

IDENTIFICATION OF MEASUREMENT SCALES

With the exception of the index of performance satisfaction, which was based on the evaluative content of written comments made after filling in the work record each day, all data on group functioning were of the external type. The initial task of data analysis is in this case the identification of the characteristics of group functioning varying over time which constitute for the group the output that it seeks to achieve, of those that are experienced and responded to as stress, etc. Each such identification has to be treated as a hypothesis to be tested. Provided that the measurement scales in terms of which the group operates have been correctly identified, the scale transformation given by the second postulate can transform the metric chosen for the construction of measurement scales into the metric in terms of which the group operates.

Application of the basic concepts defined in Chapter 5 showed, to begin with, that the group responded to time lost owing to technical breakdowns by a compensating increase in the work rate, increased performance dissatisfaction, and increased absenteeism. This finding supported the hypothesis that production-time lost was an event which had for the group the characteristics of stress, and this in turn supported the hypothesis that the rate of coal production constituted the output for the group in the sense of being one of its operative aims.

The level-of-integration scale was based on interaction-process measures given by the successive subgroupings of the team in passing from one set of tasks to the next. The interaction pattern may be represented by a partition of the team, say (AB) (CDE) (FG), showing who was working with whom at a given time, and the interaction process can be analysed in terms of subgroup splitting, fusion, and boundary changes. The minimum number of such operations required in order to transform a given interaction pattern into the succeeding one gives a measure of the transition distance, which was used to construct a measure of flexibility. The number of changes in

66

the interaction pattern per work-cycle was used to construct a measure of group-process rate.

It was found that flexibility contributed to the output rate, increased performance satisfaction, and was decreased by stress with the output rate kept constant. The group-process rate, on the other hand, contributed to a decrease in output rate and a decrease in performance satisfaction, and was increased by stress with the output rate kept constant. The two measures were therefore inversely combined to construct a level-of-integration scale.

The identification of a task-involvement measure based on group-process data was somewhat accidental. It was found that a measure of the number of team members who worked temporarily on their own during each work-cycle gave the same type of functional relationship to output, stress, and strain as did a more direct measure of task involvement employed in an earlier study (Herbst, 1957a).

In the underground situation, for a team member to work on a task temporarily isolated from other team members carries with it a special risk. It was found that isolated work occurred when a team member either went ahead to carry out preparatory work on a subsequent task in order to facilitate group progress, or finished off work on a task allowing others to go ahead.

THE DIMENSIONS OF THE VARIABLES OF GROUP FUNCTIONING

The first step in the construction of functional relationships between the variables of group functioning set out in *Table 5* is to determine the dimension of each variable.

According to the two basic postulates (Chapter 3):

All variables that refer to the internal state of a simple behaviour system can be defined in terms of the dimension [P]. Variables of dimension [P] are subject to linear scale-transformations.

67

F

All variables that refer to the transactional state of a simple behaviour system can be defined in terms of the dimension [S]. Variables of dimension [S] are subject to projective scale-transformations.

To begin with, the work rate (W), which corresponds to the rate of functioning of the activity elements of the system, and the level of integration (G), which corresponds to the inter-relationship maintained between activity elements, are both internal variables which have the dimension [P]. Level of integration can in this case be looked at as work carried out in the form of coordination of activity elements.

Under conditions of outcome predictability, the output rate (P) is completely determined by the existing work rate and level of integration, both of which are internal variables. The output rate will under these conditions be shown to be an internal variable of dimension [P].[1]

The degree of stress (S), which depends both on the internal aim-directed state of the system and on external aim-opposing events, is by definition a transactional variable which is taken to have the dimension [S].

Performance satisfaction (F) depends both on the output rate achieved (defined in terms of the performance aim of the group) and on the output rate achieved relative to the cost involved, in this case the work effort employed. These are both internal variables. Since performance satisfaction is based on two variables, namely (i) output rate and (ii) output rate relative to work effort, this suggests that it has the dimension [P^2].

Finally, task involvement (V), definable as the extent to which the system operates in an aim- and achievement-oriented way, would appear to be an internal variable, at least under conditions of outcome predictability. Strain associated with the system has been found to depend on the imbalance between output achieved

[1] However, under conditions of outcome uncertainty, output rate is a transactional variable, since the outcome is only partly under the control of the system and is partly determined by independently operating environmental systems (see Chapter 9).

and task involvement. In this case, task involvement can be expressed as a potential output rate where strain, manifested as negative affect, is zero. This implies that both variables can be measured on the same measurement scale. Task involvement is therefore taken to have the dimension $[P]$.

RATIO DIMENSIONAL ANALYSIS

The algebra of dimensions is as follows. For a dimension $[D]$

$$[D]+[D] = [D] \qquad \ldots\ldots(1)$$
$$[D]\times[D] = [D^2] \qquad \ldots\ldots(2)$$

In physics, the basic dimensions generally chosen are length, mass, and time. In this case

$$\text{length} + \text{length} = \text{length}$$
$$\text{length} \times \text{length} = \text{area}$$

By dividing a variable of dimension $[D]$ by a variable of the same dimension, we obtain

$$\frac{[D]}{[D]} = [1]$$

where $[1]$ is referred to as a non-dimensional expression.

The construction of behaviour principles is based on the additive relation of dimensions. By dividing Equation (1) by D, we obtain

$$[1]+[1] = [1]$$

which implies that the sum of two non-dimensional ratios is a non-dimensional expression. This is the prototype of behavioural equations obtained by ratio dimensional analysis.[1]

According to the theory, all relationships between behaviour variables are reducible to the form $y = f(x, z)$, that is, to relationships between three variables. We can in this case

[1] The construction of physical laws, on the other hand, is based on the multiplicative relationship. The difference appears to be due to the fact that in physics we can define new physical variables by multiplying different dimensions. This does not appear to be the case for the present set of behavioural dimensions.

construct two dimensionless ratios whose sum will be a non-dimensional quantity.

Suppose we have three variables P_1, P_2, P_3, all of which are internal variables of dimension $[P]$. By dividing, say, by P_3, we obtain two dimensionless ratios

$$\frac{P_1}{P_3} \text{ and } \frac{P_2}{P_3}$$

and the dimensional equation in this case has the form

$$f_1\left(\frac{P_1}{P_3}\right) + f_2\left(\frac{P_2}{P_3}\right) = 1$$

Since the functional form of non-dimensional variables is not yet specified, we shall make use of the following auxiliary postulate:

Postulate 3
For any set of variables which are immediate neighbours in the network of variables, the functional expression $f(x)$ in the dimensional equation can be replaced by kx, where x is a non-dimensional variable.

Provided that all three variables are directly linked in the network of behaviour variables, then, according to Postulate 3, the functional expression $f(\ )$ takes the form of a multiplicative constant. The functional relationship then takes the form

$$k_1 \frac{P_1}{P_3} + k_2 \frac{P_2}{P_3} = 1$$

Finally, according to Postulate 2, all internal variables are subject to a linear scale-transformation, so that the equation which now contains the parameters required for fitting to a given set of data is

$$k_1 \frac{a_1 P_1 + b_1}{a_3 P_3 + b_3} + k_2 \frac{a_2 P_2 + b_2}{a_3 P_3 + b_3} = 1$$

which, after simplifying, can be put in the form

$$P_1 = \alpha P_2 + \beta P_3 + \gamma$$

where α, β, γ are the parameters which need to be estimated from the data.

We can now proceed to derive the functional relationships for the present set of variables of group functioning.

The cyclic network analysis in Chapter 4 showed that

1. Output rate (P) is a direct function of work rate (W) and level of integration (G).
2. Stress (S) has a direct effect on work rate (W) and level of integration (G), and thus indirectly on output rate (P).

These, then, are the first two basic functional relationships that can be formulated.

The relationships of these variables with performance satisfaction (F) and task involvement (V) were not of a simple linear or monotonic type, so that cyclic network analysis could not be applied. The choice of a basic equation may in this case be made either on logical grounds or by identifying the simplest relationship from a data plot of the variable with every other pair of variables.

Each step in the analysis—the identification of measurement scales, the identification of the dimensions of behaviour variables, and determination of the linkage structure of variables—has to be treated as a hypothesis which becomes testable by the results obtained at a later stage of analysis. The actual research process is essentially an iteration procedure and rarely a simple linear sequence.

PRINCIPLE 1

OUTPUT RATE AS A FUNCTION OF WORK RATE AND LEVEL OF INTEGRATION

We have a set of component elements whose rates of activity, in so far as they contribute to an output rate, define the work rate of the system. By definition, no uncertainty exists about which activities lead to the output that the system operates to achieve and which activities do not. If the components operate independently and contribute to the output without loss, then the work rate of the set of components will equal the output rate, so that $P = W$. This supports the assumption that work rate and output rate must have the same dimension. Suppose, now, that the activity rates of the components are interdependent, then the output rate will depend both on the work rate and on the level of integration defined as the degree to which ongoing activity processes are effectively coordinated. In the case of individual behaviour, the level of integration corresponds to the level of skill. In the case of a work team, it corresponds to the level of coordination maintained between the team members, which is measurable in terms of the extent to which the changing pattern of work relations between team members in response to changing task conditions contributes to the output.

The definition of variables imposes the following constraints on possible functional relationships:

(i) Work rate and level of integration are restricted to positive values

$$W \geqslant 0, \qquad G \geqslant 0$$

(ii) Increases in either the work rate or the level of integration do not decrease the output rate under all conditions,

$$\left(\frac{\delta P}{\delta W}\right)_G \geqslant 0, \qquad \left(\frac{\delta P}{\delta G}\right)_W \geqslant 0,$$

for at least some positive values of W and G.

(iii) Finite degrees of work rate and integration level cannot result in an infinite output rate.

(iv) The function must be single-valued. A given work rate and integration level cannot produce two different output rates.

Let us now turn to the construction of dimensional equations. All three variables have the same dimension, and two non-dimensional expressions have to be constructed. This can be done by dividing any one variable by any other, and there are eight possible sets of ratios that can be used to construct dimensional equations. For any non-dimensional ratio $f(x)$, we set the function $f(x) = kx$.

The dimensional equations are

$$k_1 \frac{W}{P} + k_2 \frac{G}{P} = 1, \qquad \frac{1}{k_1} \frac{P}{W} + \frac{1}{k_2} \frac{P}{G} = 1, \qquad \frac{1}{k_1} \frac{P}{W} + \frac{k_1}{k_2} \frac{W}{G} = 1,$$

$$\frac{1}{k_2} \frac{P}{G} + \frac{k_2}{k_1} \frac{G}{W} = 1, \qquad k_1 \frac{W}{P} + \frac{k_2}{k_1} \frac{G}{W} = 1, \qquad k_2 \frac{G}{P} + \frac{k_1}{k_2} \frac{W}{G} = 1,$$

$$\frac{1}{k_2} \frac{P}{G} + k_1 \frac{W}{P} = 1, \qquad \frac{1}{k_1} \frac{P}{W} + \frac{1}{k_2} \frac{P}{G} = 1.$$

None of the last four equations is consistent with the constraints for any set of linear scale-transformations of variables. The first four equations are consistent with the constraints for at least some of the possible linear transformations, and when solved for P give

$$P = k_1 W + k_2 G \qquad \qquad \text{......(1a)}$$

$$P = \frac{k_1 k_2 G W}{k_1 W + k_2 G} \qquad \qquad \text{......(1b)}$$

$$P = \frac{k_1 W (k_2 G - k_1 W)}{k_2 G} \qquad \qquad \text{......(1c)}$$

$$P = \frac{k_2 G (k_1 W - k_2 G)}{k_1 W} \qquad \qquad \text{......(1d)}$$

The parameter k_1 determines the extent to which the work rate is transformed into an output rate, and k_2 determines the extent to which the coordination of activity processes contributes to the output rate. Both parameters depend on the task structure. However, in the case of group functioning, k_2 depends both on the task structure and on the chosen allocation pattern of man to task components, which defines the work organization.

We now introduce the linear transformation

$$G \to G - G_0, \quad W \to W - W_0$$

G_0, W_0, and P_0 are the zero values of the measurement scales on the basis of which the system operates. These correspond to the minimum boundary values of the system. G_0 is in this case the minimum level of integration required for the system to operate, and this has to be consistent with the minimum output rate P_0 required to satisfy survival conditions.

Substituting the linear transformations for the work rate and the level of integration, we obtain:

$$P - P_0 = k_1(W - W_0) + k_2(G - G_0) \qquad \ldots\ldots(1A)$$

$$P - P_0 = \frac{k_1 k_2 (G - G_0)(W - W_0)}{k_1(W - W_0) + k_2(G - G_0)} \qquad \ldots\ldots(1B)$$

$$P - P_0 = \frac{k_1(W - W_0)[k_2(G - G_0) - k_1(W - W_0)]}{k_2(G - G_0)} \qquad \ldots\ldots(1C)$$

$$P - P_0 = \frac{k_2(G - G_0)[k_1(W - W_0) - k_2(G - G_0)]}{k_1(W - W_0)} \qquad \ldots\ldots(1D)$$

with the restrictions on parameters

$$k_1, \ k_2, \ P_0, \ W_0, \ G_0 \geqslant 0$$

Owing to the parametric restrictions, the shape of none of the functional relationships can be changed by variations in parametric values. The relationships are shown in *Figure 9*.

The different possible relationships are clearly based on constraints deriving from the given task structure, and are to this extent invariants for different kinds of behaviour system, and this is possibly one of the few such behaviour principles that exist. Individual differences can in this case manifest themselves only with respect to the choice of the outcome criteria. Thus, given a tool and material, different persons may choose to work towards different outcomes, in which case their performances have to be measured by means of different output measures, and different work and integration measures will also be needed.

The analysis shows that four possible types of task can be distinguished. Some information about the structural and organizational characteristics of these tasks should be obtainable from the nature of the functional relationships. The following discussion will be restricted to the nature of group tasks.

Task Type A

Equation (1A) differs fundamentally from the other three in that work rate and integration level are independent as far as their contribution to the output is concerned. We note that even if the level of integration reaches its minimal value G_0, work carried out contributes to the output obtained at the same rate. Consider the effect of setting $k_2 = 0$, which abolishes all interdependence relationships. Since this condition is not inconsistent with achieving an output, it follows that the task is one that can be carried out by one person working by himself. This will be possible if there exists a sequential path through the task structure leading to the required outcome, so that one person by himself can carry out the whole task, completing one component activity after the other. This explains why this functional relationship was found in the autonomous group study. The coalmining task, although quite complex, is in fact such that it can be, and in some cases actually is, carried out by one person working on his own. However, when, as in the case of a work team, different task components are carried out by different team members, the problem of coordinating different ongoing work activities emerges in terms of scheduling, and of relocating men to task components and subgroups as the work proceeds. In this case, with $k_2 > 0$, the process of coordination and control will contribute to the output rate obtained, but will not modify the effect of the work rate on the output obtained. Integration may here be said to be extrinsic to the work rate. This, however, is not the case in any of the following types of task structure.

75

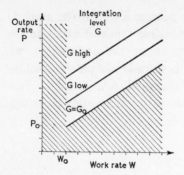

Task Type A: Any increase in work rate increases the output rate. Effective coordination contributes to the output independent of the work rate.

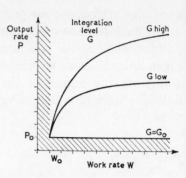

Task Type B: The existing level of integration sets a maximum to the output that can be achieved. Increasing the work rate beyond a certain point will make scarcely any contribution to the output.

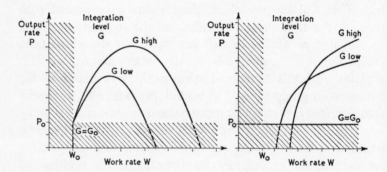

Task Type C: If the work rate exceeds the existing level of integration, the output declines, and the system collapses under overload if, with excessive work rate, the output rate goes below the minimum value P_0.

Task Type D: The higher the level of integration, the higher the work rate required if the system is to operate. If the level of integration becomes excessive relative to the work rate, the system will collapse.

FIGURE 9   OUTPUT RATE AS A FUNCTION OF WORK RATE AND LEVEL OF INTEGRATION

It should be noted that the present principle refers only to the relative contribution of work rate and level of integration to the output. With respect to output production, these two variables are independent in the Type A task. While work rate and level of integration are independent in terms of intrinsic task characteristics, they are at the same time interdependent with respect to the effect of stress as shown in Principle 2. Given the same set of scale-transformations, Principle 2 shows that, if the level of integration reaches its minimal boundary value (G_0), then the work rate also reaches its minimal boundary value (W_0).

Task Type B

We note that with $k_2 = 0$ no output results. This means that the task cannot be carried out by one person working on his own. There is therefore no sequential route of activities through the task structure. The task structure will in this case be one where a number of mutually dependent activities have to be carried on simultaneously. If a set of persons carry out mutually dependent activities, the way in which they coordinate their work will affect the work rate that they can maintain. In the Type B task, the existing level of integration sets a maximum to the output rate that can be achieved. For a given level of integration, increasing the work rate beyond a certain point will not lead to any significant increase in the output obtained, and an increased output rate can result only if the team is able to establish a higher level of work coordination.

Task Type C

Here the level of integration becomes the main determinant of output, and an optimal output results when there is a balance between work rate and the level of integration. If the work rate increases beyond this point, output decreases, and if the work rate becomes too high, the system breaks down altogether. Whereas, under the previous task condition, output is a resultant of the work rate which is facilitated by the coordination process, here the output is a resultant of the coordination process, and work rate is an input factor which has to be maintained at an appropriate level. If the work rate exceeds the amount that can be coped with by the existing level of integration, the output rate declines. We have in this case the problem of overloading, which is familiar from information theory. It may be, therefore, that there are already data available which would make it possible to test this functional relationship.

Task Type D

The functional relationship here, which in a sense is the reverse of Type C, has the peculiar property that, with a given work rate, an excessive level of integration decreases the output rate. I am not sure under which task conditions this would apply. We may have to wait until empirical verification of the relationship becomes available in order to find out to which type of task structure, if any, the relationship applies. Alternatively, we may have to exclude by definition the possibility that the level of integration can decrease the output rate.

There is, finally, a fifth equation that satisfies the basic constraints, which is obtained by multiplying the non-dimensional variables and has the form $P = \sqrt{k_1 k_2 WG}$. The relationship has some similarity to the Type B task. There is some doubt in this case with respect to the meaningfulness of defining a $[P^{\frac{1}{2}}]$ dimensional variable. $[P^2]$, on the other hand, is the dimension associated with performance-evaluation variables and not with performance variables.

PRINCIPLE 2

EFFECT OF STRESS ON WORK RATE
AND LEVEL OF INTEGRATION

This relationship is particularly easy to derive. Work rate (W) and level of integration (G) both have the dimension $[P]$. These two variables can therefore be put in the non-dimensional form $\frac{W}{b_1 G}$. Stress (S), as a transactional variable, enters the relationship in a non-dimensional projective form which we denote by

$$\rho(S) = \frac{\alpha S + \beta}{\gamma S + \delta}$$

We note that adding a constant to a projective function, or inverting it, leaves the projective form of the expression unchanged. The dimensional equation in this case is

$$\frac{W}{b_1 G} + \rho_1(S) = 1 \qquad \qquad \ldots\ldots(2a)$$

so that

$$\frac{W}{b_1 G} = 1 - \rho_1(S) = \rho_2(S) \qquad \qquad \ldots\ldots(2b)$$

This is the only relationship consistent with the postulates, since inverting the expression on either side does not lead to a different functional form.

Applying the linear transformation $W \rightarrow W - W_0$, $G \rightarrow G - G_0$, and writing out the projective expression

$$\rho_2(S) = \frac{b_4 S + b_5}{b_6 S + b_7}$$

we arrive at

$$W - W_0 = b_1(G - G_0)\frac{b_4 S + b_5}{b_6 S + b_7} \qquad \qquad \ldots\ldots(2c)$$

which is the generalized form of the relationship.

The expression can be simplified if we set

$$\frac{b_1 b_4}{b_6} = e, \quad \frac{b_5}{b_4} = c, \quad \text{and} \quad \frac{b_7}{b_6} = d$$

so that

$$W - W_0 = e(G - G_0)\frac{S + c}{S + d} \qquad \qquad \ldots\ldots(2d)$$

Work rate and level of integration intersect at the minimal boundary values $W = W_0$ and $G = G_0$.

There are no obvious restrictions on the values that may be taken by the parameters other than that there must be conditions where both work rate and level of integration have values above their minimal boundary levels $W \geqslant W_0$, $G \geqslant G_0$, and $b_1 [\rho_2(S)] > 0$. However, there will be some parametric conditions which transform the stress variable into its inverse, which is support, and these conditions are not yet specifiable. Although there is a considerable literature on the effects of stress, there are so far scarcely any comparable studies on the dynamics of support and help relations.

We may now consider a special case of this function. If $d > c > o$ and $e > 0$, then we have the relationship found in the autonomous group study. This has the property that:

1. Under conditions of stress, the work rate increases or the level of integration decreases or both effects occur simultaneously.
2. If integration is maintained constant, then stress increases the work rate up to a limiting value, and the higher the level of integration, the higher the limiting value achieved.

There is no difficulty in mapping out the family of functional relationships obtained by varying the parametric values. At least one of these is of a linear form if $b_6 = 0$. However, as already noted, some transformations of the stress variable will convert it into a support variable. Suppose, for instance, instead of $d > c$ as before, we have $c > d$. In this case, stress increases the level of integration and decreases the work rate, and from the next principle this condition is related to increasing performance satisfaction. This is the type of response that would be expected if the relationship is perceived as an aim-supporting rather than as an aim-interfering and stressful one.

PRINCIPLE 3

PERFORMANCE SATISFACTION AS A
FUNCTION OF OUTPUT RATE AND WORK RATE

Under conditions of outcome predictability, work rate and level of integration are the only factors on which variations in the output depend. Performance satisfaction can be expressed as a function of the output achieved relative to the work rate employed. From Principle 1, output and work rate fully determine the concurrent level of integration. This means, however, that there will be consistency requirements between the characteristics of the task structure, given by the form taken by Principle 1, and the performance-satisfaction function.

The minimal constraints that have to be put on the dimensional equation are:

1. The function should be single-valued with respect to performance satisfaction.
2. With $W \geqslant W_0$ and $P \geqslant P_0$, performance satisfaction must be able to take positive, neutral, and negative values with at least one set of scale-transformations.

Since performance satisfaction (F) has the dimension $[P^2]$, the possible sets of non-dimensional variables are as follows:

$$\frac{F}{gP^2}, \quad \frac{fW}{P}, \quad \frac{F}{gf^2W^2},$$

together with their inverses, which give ten dimensional equations that are consistent with the given constraints. The performance-satisfaction function is likely to be different for tasks that primarily involve work effort and for those that primarily involve coordination. The function consistent with the Type A task in the autonomous group study is obtained from the first two ratios

$$\frac{F}{gP^2} + \frac{fW}{P} = 1 \qquad \qquad ......(3a)$$

so that

$$F = gP(P - fW) \qquad \qquad ......(3b)$$

and with the corresponding linear transformation $W \rightarrow W - W_0$, $P \rightarrow P - P_0$, we obtain

$$F = g(P - P_0)[(P - P_0) - f(W - W_0)] \qquad ......(3c)$$

with $g, f > 0$. Performance satisfaction in this case increases both with the output obtained and with the degree to which the output rate is high relative to the work effort employed. We may identify f as a performance-expectation parameter, since the higher f is, the greater is the output rate needed relative to the work rate employed to achieve a given level of performance satisfaction. To provide consistency with the Type A task, the performance-expectation parameter has to exceed the ease with which the task can be carried out by a certain amount in order to provide conditions for performance dissatisfaction, that is, $f > k_1$, where k_1 is the task parameter in Principle 1A.

PRINCIPLE 6

OUTPUT RATE AS A FUNCTION OF STRESS AND TASK INVOLVEMENT

The derivation of Principle 6 is identical with that of Principle 2. Output rate and task involvement both have the dimension $[P]$ and stress enters into the relationship in a projective form. The relationship can thus be written down straight away in the form

$$\frac{P}{c_1 V} = \frac{c_2 S + c_3}{c_4 S + c_5} \qquad \ldots\ldots(6a)$$

Output rate and task involvement have in this case a point of intersection. The available empirical evidence shows that minimal task involvement is not essential for output maintenance so that the previous linear transformations do not necessarily apply. With the transformation

$$P \to P - P_c \quad \text{and} \quad V \to V - V_c$$

the point of intersection is moved within the range of system-functioning, and we obtain

$$P - P_c = c_1 (V - V_c) \frac{c_2 S + c_3}{c_4 S + c_5} \qquad \ldots\ldots(6b)$$

The possible forms of the relationship depend on the parametric values taken by the projective form of the stress function. So far, only one form of the relationship has been empirically established, which is obtained by setting

$$\frac{c_3}{c_2} = -S_c, \quad \frac{c_5}{c_4} = k, \quad \frac{c_1 c_2}{c_4} = -n$$

giving

$$P - P_c = n(V - V_c)\frac{S_c - S}{S + k} \qquad \qquad \ldots\ldots(6c)$$

In this case, with low involvement ($V < V_c$), stress increases the output rate, but if involvement exceeds this critical value ($V > V_c$), then stress decreases the output rate. V_c is here identifiable as the frustration threshold.

P_c represents an output level which can be maintained constant irrespective of the degree of stress (at least within a certain range), and this condition results if the involvement level is kept precisely at the frustration threshold level ($V = V_c$).

S_c is identifiable as the stress threshold. If stress is below this level ($S < S_c$), increasing task involvement increases the output rate, whereas above the threshold level ($S > S_c$), increasing task involvement decreases the output rate. Task involvement may in this case be looked at as mediating the effect of stress on the work rate and level of integration (Principle 2), which in turn determine the output rate obtained (Principle 1).

Each individual principle thus has to be considered with respect to the larger network of relations within which it operates and with which it has to be consistent. A set of four principles found in the autonomous group study has been shown to be derivable as a special case. The task structure has been found to play a central role and to operate as a constraint on the possible type of behaviour system that can evolve. A given task structure will be consistent with a specific range of behaviour networks. Switching over to a different task structure will provide the basis for a different range of behaviour networks. The mapping out of these relationships, which are of particular relevance to the study of socio-technical systems, will require a good deal of empirical research.

When we compare the behaviour principles that operate

83

under conditions of outcome predictability with those that operate under conditions of outcome uncertainty, discussed in the following chapters, we find that, under conditions of outcome uncertainty, the greater range of variation in dimensional equations, the greater independence of parameters, and, particularly, the greater range that can be taken by parametric values, provide a condition where each behavioural universe can acquire a unique set of behavioural laws. Under conditions of outcome predictability, however, the specific constraints deriving from the task structure reduce the possible range of variation considerably, and create a condition where relatively more uniform networks of behaviour principles can emerge. The distinction here is related to the differences in dynamic structure between the fantasy and future perspective level of the life-space and the reality level discussed by Lewin. The analysis also supports one of the points made by Marcuse (1964), that a highly developed technology, or, perhaps more precisely, commitment to the operation of a technological system, is a significant source of behavioural uniformity which can be effective quite apart from explicit normative pressure.

CHAPTER 7

The Pupil and his Task
The Cross-sectional Case-study Technique

————◆————

SUMMARY

The cross-sectional case-study technique provided for the first time the possibility of testing behaviour principles on the basis of a larger number of cases. Unlike the longitudinal technique, which makes use of the possibility of studying behaviour on a single task over time, the cross-sectional technique is based on the possibility of studying the behaviour of a person on a number of simultaneous tasks.

The method is applied to the study of pupil-task relationships at school. For each school subject, measures are obtained concerning work effort, performance expectation, and emotional response. All measures concerned with the pupils' perception of the existing situation are based on a quantal intensity scale. Measures of performance expectation, in terms of examination results, require the construction of an outcome probability and an outcome uncertainty scale.

————◆————

ALL QUANTITATIVE case-study techniques are based on the possibility of obtaining data relating to the same system under a sufficiently wide range of different conditions.

The state of a system at a given time is given by a set of behaviour variables x, y, z, which are directly measured, and a set of structural parameters α_1, α_2, α_3 . . ., which appear in the functional relationship between variables

$$f(x,y,z,\alpha_1,\alpha_2,\alpha_3, \ldots) = 0$$

The system is said to remain the same if all parameters remain unchanged. Since all parameters are potentially subject to

85

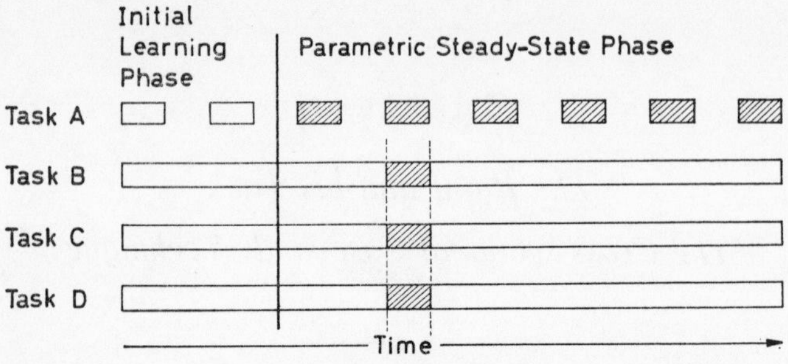

FIGURE 10 THE LONGITUDINAL AND CROSS-SECTIONAL TECHNIQUES

The cross-hatched areas along the horizontal axis show the set of measures obtained in the longitudinal case-study technique. The cross-hatched areas down the vertical axis show the set of measures obtained in the cross-sectional technique.

change, we speak in this case of a parametric steady-state condition.

To obtain a wide range of different conditions requires that all behaviour variables vary as widely as possible within their potential range of values, when system parameters have acquired steady-state values.

Figure 10 contrasts the longitudinal and the cross-sectional case-study techniques. In both cases, measurement is started after completion of the initial learning phase.

The longitudinal technique is based on measures obtained for a single repetitive task. It is possible in this case to employ external physicalist-type measures which at the stage of data analysis can be transformed into the measurement scales in terms of which the system operates.

The cross-sectional technique is based on measures obtained for a set of tasks all of which are carried out at the same time and under the same conditions. Measures are obtained for each task on a set of variables $(x, y, z \ldots)$. Provided that the same parametric values apply to all tasks, the set of measures obtained for each task $(x_1 y_1 z_1 \ldots), (x_2 y_2 z_2 \ldots) \ldots (x_n y_n z_n \ldots)$ can be treated as different possible states of the same system.

Table 6 shows the type of data obtained by means of the cross-sectional technique in a study of pupil-task relationships at

TABLE 6 BASIC DATA: THE CASE OF ELLY

Subject	Variable					
	Anxiety X	Work effort required W_n	Work effort W	Boredom B	Performance expectation P_e	Outcome uncertainty U
English	3	2	2	1	2·20	·44
Mathematics	3	1	1	0	3·49	·32
German	2	1	1	1	2·96	·28
History	1	1	1	1	3·13	·15
Physics	1	2	1	3	2·84	·55
Norwegian (riksmål)	1	0	0	0	3·49	·12
Geography	0	0	0	1	3·40	·10
Nature Study	0	0	0	2	3·18	·10
Religion	0	0	0	2	3·30	·10
Norwegian (nynorsk)	0	1	0	3	2·94	·44

school. For each school subject that pupils have to take in the course of the year, measures were obtained on a set of variables concerned with work effort, emotional response, and performance expectation.

The data obtained for Elly, which have already been discussed in Chapter 4, will later on be analysed systematically together with material obtained from other cases.

Before presenting the measurement technique employed, we shall need to consider the problems involved in the construction of subjective measurement scales.

INTENSITY SCALES

Our experiences of phenomena such as pleasure, satisfaction with a task well done, effort devoted to solving a problem, anxiety about possible future events, can vary quantitatively in intensity. Intensity cannot, however, be measured on a continuous infinitely divisible scale. Experienced satisfaction, say, cannot be meaningfully expressed in terms of figures taken to several decimal places. Nor is a set theoretical scale possible, since experienced intensity does not correspond to an accumulation of experientally definable elementary units.[1]

One possible starting-off point is to note the form in which experienced intensities are communicated. Here we find an almost universal linguistic scale, which can be put in the form (i) none, (ii) a little, mild, or fairly, (iii) very, and (N) extremely. This suggests that intensity is measurable in terms of a four-point scale which corresponds to quantal intensity levels or, perhaps better, intensity bands. Intensity levels are generally distinguishable not only quantitatively but also qualitatively. Being mildly happy or unhappy differs from being extremely happy or unhappy, not only in intensity, but to some extent both in the qualitative nature of the experience and in its behavioural and possible physiological concomitants.

[1] In the observational study of animal behaviour (and possibly in the study of human behaviour as well), however, quantal intensity scales can be constructed, based on the number of successive activity components that come into operation (Russell, Mead, and Hayes, 1954).

The problem we need to consider first is that of the conditions under which a scale of this type can be used for plotting and testing functional relationships between behaviour variables.

The basic hypothesis is that there is a finite number of experienced intensity levels. The number of scale points on the measurement scale has to correspond with the number of experienced intensity levels. Our specific assumption at this stage is that there are four subjective intensity levels, at least under conditions where there is no physical external referent.

We designate the intensity levels by

none	fairly, a little	very	extremely
0	1	2	3

associating the scale points with the integral values 0, 1, 2, 3. All characteristics of tasks and activities are to be measured by the *same* scale. However, we have no reason to assume that the numerical scale values will correspond to the intensity scale on which a given person operates either in terms of interval distances, because the distances between successive intensity levels may be unequal, or in terms of the zero point, because the 'none' category will not necessarily correspond to the operative zero point of the scale. Thus it is conceivable that the basic anxiety level of a particular person is, say, fairly anxious. Also, we have already previously seen that the operative zero point for an output scale corresponds to an output quantity which is just sufficient to maintain the survival of the system. Furthermore, the scale values cannot be assumed to have the same metrical properties for different behavioural variables. Thus the intensity scales for, say, anxiety and work effort may have different zero points and different scale intervals.

Now, according to the first two postulates, we are dealing with two types of variable. These are internal variables, which are subject to linear scale-transformations, and transactional variables, which are subject to projective scale-transformations. These scale-transformations are built into the functional relationships. In the case of the autonomous group study discussed in Chapter 6, the external physicalist measurement scales employed have equal-interval properties and the functional equations can then take care of the necessary scale-transformations. In the case of subjective intensity scales, however, we do not have information on interval distances.

With regard to subjective scales as used in this study, there are a number of alternative possibilities:

1. It is shown in Chapter 8 that all variables can be put in the form of projective expressions. However, no technique exists as yet for the construction of non-metric projective scales. These might be based on the invariance property of the harmonic ratio.[1]

2. No behaviourally relevant information is lost through the use of ordinal instead of metric scales. However, we do not yet have an algebra for ordinal functional relationships that can be used for fitting data.

3. Behavioural variables cannot as a rule be taken to be continuously distributed but will appear in quantal intensity levels. In this case a rating-scale will be an appropriate measure, provided the number of scale points does not exceed the number of distinguishable quantal intensity levels. If intensity levels are clearly distinguishable this means that they are at least well spaced, so that each quantal level will lie somewhere near the midpoint of the immediately superior and inferior levels. Suppose that, to begin with, we use an intensity scale as an approximate equal-interval scale, then, at the next stage, it would be possible to use the theoretical relationships for the purpose of scale calibration.

Each of these possibilities would be worth further investigation. In the present study a fourth alternative was chosen as a

[1] The linear scale-transformation is a special case of the projective transformation. For a projective transformation, the value of any three points can be arbitrarily chosen. The choice of a fourth point implies the specification of a fixed harmonic ratio. If a set of four points is to be convertible to an equal-interval scale by means of a projective transformation, the harmonic ratio must have the value $-\frac{1}{2}$.

transitional technique. The available data show that, provided the same intensity scale is used for measuring each variable, no serious discrepancies are observed in fitting algebraic functions. The restriction has to be accepted, however, that no inferences should be made with respect to relationships between variables that cannot be made from an ordinal scale, and, moreover, that no inferences may be made from parametric values beyond that of parametric inequalities which determine the direction of the relationships. Since integral values are used for scale points, parameters used for fitting are restricted to integral values.

There is one problem that remains. Our basic data are a finite number of quantal levels associated with the integral values 0, 1, 2, 3 respectively. However, theoretically predicted values are not restricted to whole-number values. There are two possibilities. We could employ an algebra which would generate only integral values; this would imply a severe restriction on possible parametric values. The alternative is to assume that the actual value will be the nearest integral value.

Finally, it is worth while keeping in mind that the interval distance between intensity levels as such is not an important problem. The prediction problem we are concerned with is, for instance, given that the intensity levels for variables X and Y are 1 and 3 respectively, to determine the intensity level for variable Z. Provided with an array of data of this type we could, if we wished, look for a set of interval distances that would bring the relationships into their simplest and most convenient form. It could, in fact, be worth while to consider this possibility at the stage of data analysis.

PROBABILITY SCALES

Under the condition of outcome uncertainty, which exists for a pupil in the school situation, task behaviour will be related to an expected outcome. Provided that the examination grade received is accepted as a personally relevant outcome criterion, all performance measures related to the expected outcome involve a probability estimate. The method that will be used is to ask for a likelihood estimate for each possible examination grade, which may be A, B, C, D, or F. The distribution obtained resembles a probability curve with the likelihood decreasing as we move away from the modal value.

There are in this case a number of scale values which would appear to be given by definition. The pupil may judge a given examination grade in a particular subject to be:

1. Impossible: the probability estimate is zero and the uncertainty estimate is zero.
2. Quite certain: probability is one and uncertainty is zero.
3. Possible, in the sense that it could happen or could not happen: probability is ·5 and uncertainty is one.

On linguistic grounds there are at least two intermediate probability levels; these correspond to 'unlikely' and 'very likely' respectively. If we take the estimation scale to be symmetrical, then, if the probability estimate for 'unlikely' is X, the value for 'very likely' becomes $1 - X$. The value of X might be chosen to be between ·1 and ·2.

The results obtained show that the sum of probabilities over all possible performance outcomes is scarcely ever unity for any reasonable assumption that can be made about estimate values. The values obtained tend to lie between 2 and 2·5.

If the sum of probabilities obtained is, say, 2, then a probability scale ranging from zero to unity can be obtained by dividing the probability estimates by 2. With the value $X = ·2$, the adjusted probability values would be

impossible	unlikely	possible	very likely	quite certain
0	·1	·25	·4	·5

If a person tells us that he is 'quite certain' about a grade, this does not necessarily mean what it seems to mean. It refers in the above case to a marked peak of the probability distribution, and thus to an outcome that is considerably more likely than most other outcomes, and has certainty only in this sense. A pupil may, for instance, judge that he is practically certain to get a B grade, but, since there are many sources of uncertainty related to his personal performance, the types of examination question given, the personal judgement of the examiner, and so on, the possibility of bad luck with respect to any of these will still leave a relatively high probability for a C grade. Some possibility may still be left over for a relatively more unlikely A or D grade.

Complete certainty in the mathematical sense will correspond to a judgement that one outcome is certain and *all* other outcomes are impossible. Probability measures have therefore to be based on probability estimates for all possible outcomes. The probability estimates will in the following be used to provide two types of expected outcome measure. One of these is the expected performance level. The other is the degree of outcome uncertainty, which will have a maximum value if all grades are judged to be equally possible and a minimum value if one grade is judged to be quite certain while all other grades are judged to be impossible.

The variables selected for measurement are based on the concepts that define the functioning of behaviour systems. The set of concepts and the corresponding type of measure employed are shown below.

Conceptual variable	*Measure*
Activity rate	Work effort Work effort required
Task involvement (action potential)	Desire for success
Strain and balance	Boredom Interest Like—Dislike
Transactional variables	Expected examination grade Anxiety about examination grade
Performance satisfaction	Performance satisfaction Performance evaluation
Outcome probability variables	Outcome uncertainty Probability of success, of failure, and of indifferent outcome Success and failure expectation

93

BASIC VARIABLES

A. CHARACTERISTICS OF SCHOOL SUBJECTS

All basic variables concerned with the characteristics of school subjects are measured by the four-point intensity scale

none	fairly	very	extremely
0	1	2	3

Thus, to measure desire for success, the question used is: 'How important is it for you to do particularly well in this subject?' The intensity scale takes the form

extremely important	very important	fairly important	not important

Pupils were then asked to rank subjects. The question used was: 'Suppose you can get an A grade in only one subject. Starting with the subjects you have marked with a cross in the column "extremely important", put a 1 after the cross for the subject which you would most like to get an A grade in, etc.'

It was thought that the additional ranking might provide a finer differentiation of the scale. This, however, did not appear to be the case. Quite consistently, the best results in data analysis are obtained by the quantal intensity scales. However, the additional ranking can be used as a consistency check. The basic variables are as follows:

1. *Boredom* (B)

How boring do you find each subject?

2. *Anxiety* (X)

How worried are you about examination results in each subject?

3. *Work Effort Required* (W_n)

How much work do you have to put into each subject in order to get a good result?

94

4. *Work Effort* (*W*)

How much work do you generally put into each subject?

B. MEASUREMENT OF PERFORMANCE EXPECTATION

The data obtained for the measurement of performance expectation and outcome uncertainty are as shown in *Table 7*.

For major subjects (languages and mathematics), pupils can receive one of five possible grades in their final examination:

Grade	A	B	C	D	F
	extremely good	very good	satisfactory	poor	fail
Grade scale (*g*)	1	2	3	4	5

In the remaining minor subjects, possible grades range from B to F.

For each subject, pupils were asked how likely it was that they would get an A grade, a B grade, etc.

	im-possible	unlikely	possible	very likely	quite certain
Probability scale (*p**)	0	·2	·5	·8	1·0
Uncertainty scale (*u*)	0	·2	1·0	·2	0

Since the probability estimates do not sum to unity, a probability measure *p*, ranging from zero to unity, is constructed by dividing each probability estimate obtained by the sum of the estimates:

$$\text{Probability measure, } p = \frac{p^*}{\Sigma p^*}$$

Next, the pupil was asked: 'Suppose that you were to get an A grade (B grade, etc.), how would you feel about this?' The alternatives he was instructed to use were:

	extremely happy	very happy	fairly happy	don't care	fairly upset	very upset	extremely upset
Response scale (*v*)	+3	+2	+1	0	−1	−2	−3

TABLE 7 DATA SHEET AND MEASURES OBTAINED FOR ELLY'S GERMAN EXAMINATION

Examination grade g	Response	v	Impossible	Unlikely	Possible	Very likely	Quite certain	p*	u	p	gp	p_s	p_f	vp
A 5	Extremely happy	+3	x					0	0	0	0	0	0	0
B 4	Extremely happy	+3				x		·8	·2	·32	1·28	·32		+·96
C 3	Fairly happy	+1					x	1·0	0	·40	1·20	·40		+·40
D 2	Very upset	−2			x			·5	1·0	·20	·40		·20	−·40
F 1	Extremely upset	−3		x				·2	·2	·08	·08		·08	−·24
Sum (Σ)								2·5	1·4	1·00	2·96	·72	·28	·64
											P_e	E_s 1·36	E_f	

There are a large number of possible measures that can be constructed on the basis of this technique. In the present study, only two measures were employed for more intensive analysis. The data and computation sheet for Elly's German examination are shown in *Table 7*.

Both of the basic variables that will be used are obtained from the first two scales. These are:

5. *Outcome Uncertainty* (*U*)

Complete outcome certainty would exist if each grade was marked either impossible or certain. Complete uncertainty will exist if all grades are regarded as having equally possible outcomes.

Using the above *u* scale, we obtain

$$\text{Outcome uncertainty, } U = \frac{\Sigma u}{n}$$

where *n* is the number of possible grades; in the present case $n = 5$.

Thus, for Elly, outcome uncertainty with regard to her German examination is

$$U = \frac{1 \cdot 4}{5} = \cdot 28$$

The uncertainty measure ranges from zero in the case of complete certainty to unity in the case of complete outcome uncertainty.

No case of outcome certainty for any pupil on any subject was found. This provides full support for the basic assumption that the school situation is one of outcome uncertainty for all pupils.

6. *Performance Expectation* (*P_e*)

The grade value *g* is multiplied by the achievement probability *p*:

$$\text{Performance expectation, } P_e = \Sigma gp$$

97

AUXILIARY VARIABLES

A number of auxiliary variables were included in the study, some of which measure the same variables in a somewhat different form. Also, it was desired to test the properties of a bipolar scale which has the form

| extremely negative | very negative | fairly negative | neutral | fairly positive | very positive | extremely positive |

The reason for excluding these variables from the more detailed analysis in the following chapters is briefly noted.

Desire for Success

How important is it for you to do particularly well in this subject? (Unipolar scale.)

Few simple relationships are found with any of the other variables. Consistent with findings from the autonomous group study, functional plots generally give a family of U-shaped curves. The only known linear-type relationship of a task-involvement variable with oppositional stress and outcome achieved is discussed in Chapter 6.

Difficulty

How difficult do you find each subject to be? (Bipolar scale ranging from 'extremely easy' to 'extremely difficult'.)

This scale was regarded as a possible alternative to the 'work effort needed' scale. It was excluded because it turned out to be essential to use the same scale for all variables. It is in any case an advantage to measure work effort and work effort needed on the same scale since, as a special case, the relationship can reduce to $W = W_n$, which leads to simpler possible functional forms.

Performance Evaluation

How well do you feel you are doing in each subject? (Bipolar scale ranging from 'well' to 'badly'.)

Pupils receive progress grades at the end of each term so that a basis for performance evaluation exists. Relationships to other variables are generally monotonic.

Performance Satisfaction

How satisfied are you with the results obtained in each subject? (Bipolar scale ranging from 'satisfied' to 'dissatisfied'.)

The relationship of performance satisfaction to work effort and output rate under conditions of outcome predictability is discussed in Chapter 6. Under conditions of outcome predictability, performance level is entirely a function of the person's own effort. In the present case, where grades received have no necessary relation to effort and skill, and where self-evaluation is not necessarily based on examination grades received, the problem of finding for each pupil a basis for accounting for his performance satisfaction appears to be more difficult.

Interest

How interesting do you feel each subject is? (Unipolar scale.)

Boredom and interest are independent variables, at least in so far as some aspects of the situation may be positive and others negative. The indications so far are that negative variables such as boredom, anxiety, stress, etc. are linked to performance variables by simpler functional structures than are positive variables. There are two possibilities. Either the relations between positive variables and behaviour are more complex, or, and this seems more likely, the behaviour of most schoolchildren in our culture is more directly linked to negative emotionality than to positive feelings.

99

H

Liking

How much do you like each subject? (Bipolar scale ranging from 'extreme dislike' to 'extreme liking'.)

This is, of course, an invalid type of scale since liking and dislike are independent variables. However, attitudes are frequently forced along this type of scale and it seemed interesting to take it along.

Success and Failure Expectation

The simplest types of measure that can be constructed are

Success probability p_s	= sum of probabilities of positive outcome expectations
Failure probability p_f	= sum of probabilities of negative outcome expectations
Indifferent outcome probability p_o	= sum of probabilities of don't care outcome

$$p_s + p_f + p_o = 1$$

Of these measures, the probability of an indifferent outcome, or, conversely, the probability of an emotional response, provides the most interesting relationships. However, the frequency distribution of this measure is for most individuals too narrow to be of use.

For exploratory purposes, an alternative measure shown in *Table 7* was constructed, taking account of the intensity of emotional response.

Success expectation $E_s = \Sigma |vp|$ for positive outcome values

Failure expectation $E_f = \Sigma |vp|$ for negative outcome values

From an examination of the basic data it seems clear that there is a meaningful pattern in the probability of grades and emotional responses. Contrary to expectations, however, it is found that the relationships of success and failure measures to other variables do not appear to be of a simple type.

PILOT TEST

An opportunity for pilot-testing the technique became available unexpectedly when the Institute for Industrial Social Research at Trondheim was approached by the director of the local School of Social Work, who was looking for a way to obtain data from students for an evaluation of the school's curriculum. Arrangements were made for a staff member of the Institute, who was also a teacher at the school, to undertake the administration. The data obtained were to be analysed and evaluated by the teaching staff of the school and this was known to the students. No attempt to maintain anonymity was made.

The initial administration was thus made under conditions in which one would expect the least reliable data. What happened was that quite a large number of students filled in the questionnaire, especially the evaluative scales, without providing any information whatever. This is easily done by stating that all subjects are liked fairly well, or liked very much. When Shannon's measure is applied, the amount of information provided is found to be zero.

The results obtained suggested a number of useful indications. It could be concluded that the chances of obtaining systematically distorted data are quite small since it is much easier to furnish data that give no information whatsoever. At the same time, to the extent that this does happen, the students provide us with the information that the conditions under which the data are acquired are unsatisfactory.

The school itself felt that the data collected were useful, since, at the level of population analysis, sufficient discrimination was secured.

THE SCHOOL STUDY

A major requirement for the study of individual cases was that data should be obtained for the maximum possible number of subjects in which formal examinations are taken at the end of a school year. This excluded the choice of university studies, which in Norway are highly specialized. It is in the ninth grade at school that the maximum number of subjects has to be taken at the same time, the age-range of the pupils being fourteen to fifteen. Two classes at different schools in Trondheim were chosen. It turned out that academic achievement in Class A was relatively low, and that there had been quite a large number of failures in previous examinations. In Class B academic achievement was appreciably higher, partly because the school concerned takes in a large proportion of the children of the staff at the local technical university. The administration was carried out about four months before the final examinations, early in 1964.

The purpose of the study was explained to pupils as follows:

'A research group at the Technical University is at present engaged in a study of the kinds of problem that secondary school pupils have with their work at school. What we hope to find out is which subjects pupils like and which subjects they dislike, which subjects they feel are difficult and which they consider easy. By finding out how you feel about this, we hope to be able to make recommendations about possible ways of improving the curriculum and teaching methods. It is therefore important that you answer all questions as exactly as you can. At the same time, we don't want you to think too much about each question; just write down what you feel about these things at this moment. Your answers will under no conditions be made available to your school, any of your teachers, or your parents.'

Unlike the pilot test, the results obtained, including the evaluative scales, gave no indication that information was withheld by means of undifferentiated responses.

For the purpose of a preliminary analysis, a correlation matrix was calculated based on the characteristics of tasks (school subjects). The information utilized in this case consisted of the relative characteristics of school subjects. With the exception of the success and failure expectation measures, the correlation matrices for the two classes are practically identical (*Table 8*). It can be concluded that, at least at the population level, the measurement technique has a high degree of reliability.

McQuitty linkage analysis shows the existence of three identical clusters with the exception of the 'work effort required' variable. Moreover, the same basic linkage structure is found within each cluster (*Figure 11*). The results obtained were confirmed by means of hierarchical linkage analysis.[1]

The three clusters obtained have some similarity to those found in semantic differential data:

Cluster 1 consists of task involvement and work effort variables:
   desire for success, anxiety about examination results, failure expectation, work effort.

Cluster 2 consists of task valence variables:
   interest, boredom, liking, success expectation, indifferent outcome probability.

Cluster 3 consists of performance expectation and performance evaluation variables:
   performance expectation, performance satisfaction, performance evaluation, difficulty, outcome uncertainty.

It is apparent that work effort is closely linked to anxiety, desire for success, and expectation of failure, and that positive affect, such as interest and success expectation, plays a secondary role. This is consistent with what is known about Norwegian schools. In spite of an ideology to encourage the development of interest in the task, what counts in practice is the grade received in the written examination. The major incentive employed is anxiety and the main inhibitor is boredom. In these circumstances, the strategy that can most easily be exploited by a teacher is to combat boredom by increasing anxiety about examination results, since this will, at the same time, lead to increased work effort.

1 I am indebted to Dosent Thor Paasche for the statistical analysis.

TABLE 8   MATRIX OF CORRELATION

		Work effort W	Anxiety X	Work effort required W_n	Desire for success D_s	Failure expectation E_f	Difficulty D
Work effort	W	x	·97 ·92	·93 ·83	·94 ·93	·76 ·76	·77 ·60
Anxiety	X	·97 ·92	x	·97 ·89	·94 ·91	·75 ·73	·87 ·77
Work effort required	W_n	·93 ·83	·97 ·89	x	·89 ·82	·75 ·55	·94 ·93
Desire for success	D_s	·94 ·93	·94 ·91	·89 ·82	x	·83 ·69	·75 ·65
Failure expectation	E_f	·76 ·76	·75 ·73	·75 ·55	·83 ·69	x	·67 ·30
Difficulty	D	·77 ·60	·87 ·77	·94 ·93	·75 ·65	·67 ·30	x
Performance evaluation	P_r	− ·60 − ·70	− ·75 − ·84	− ·83 − ·97	− ·61 − ·74	− ·60 − ·43	− ·95 − ·98
Performance satisfaction	F	− ·63 − ·61	− ·79 − ·79	− ·83 − ·89	− ·67 − ·66	− ·65 − ·33	− ·93 − ·96
Outcome uncertainty	U	·42 ·61	·51 ·69	·64 ·73	·38 ·56	·20 ·43	·67 ·68
Performance expectation	P_e	− ·64 − ·62	− ·74 − ·75	− ·83 − ·93	− ·57 − ·58	− ·70 − ·46	− ·94 − ·92
Interest	I	·69 ·78	·59 ·56	·53 ·45	·51 ·73	·28 ·64	·35 ·14
Boredom	B	− ·77 − ·80	− ·66 − ·56	− ·58 − ·47	− ·63 − ·73	− ·44 − ·70	− ·36 − ·13
Liking	L	·74 ·83	·62 ·62	·58 ·50	·63 ·76	·47 ·73	·31 ·16
Probability of indifferent outcome	p_o	− ·53 − ·68	− ·34 − ·50	− ·23 − ·24	− ·43 − ·65	− ·24 − ·59	·08 ·05
Success expectation	E_s	·12 ·35	− ·03 ·26	− ·08 ·19	− ·09 − ·37	− ·41 − ·08	− ·30 ·08

The top row of figures shows the results obtained for Class A; the second row

Performance evaluation P_r	Performance satisfaction F	Outcome uncertainty U	Performance expectation P_e	Interest I	Boredom B	Liking L	Probability of indifferent outcome p_o	Success expectation E_s
− ·60	− ·63	·42	− ·64	·69	− ·77	·74	− ·53	·12
− ·70	− ·61	·61	− ·62	·78	− ·80	·83	− ·68	·35
− ·75	− ·79	·51	− ·74	·59	− ·66	·62	− ·34	− ·03
− ·84	− ·79	·69	− ·75	·56	− ·56	·62	− ·50	·26
− ·83	− ·83	·64	− ·83	·53	− ·58	·58	− ·23	− ·08
− ·97	− ·89	·73	− ·93	·45	− ·47	·50	− ·24	·19
− ·61	− ·67	·38	− ·57	·51	− ·63	·63	− ·43	− ·09
− ·74	− ·66	·56	− ·58	·73	− ·73	·76	− ·65	− ·37
− ·60	− ·65	·20	− ·70	·28	− ·44	·47	− ·24	− ·41
− ·43	− ·33	·43	− ·46	·64	− ·70	·73	− ·59	− ·08
− ·95	− ·93	·67	− ·94	·35	− ·36	·31	·08	− ·30
− ·98	− ·96	·68	− ·92	·14	− ·13	·16	·05	·08
x	·98	− ·63	·94	− ·18	·19	− ·14	− ·31	·48
	·96	− ·68	·94	− ·24	·25	− ·29	·09	− ·07
·98	x	− ·57	·90	− ·16	·19	− ·15	− ·28	·50
·96		− ·65	·89	− ·06	·08	− ·13	·08	− ·02
− ·63	− ·57	x	− ·49	·28	− ·16	·06	·01	·15
− ·68	− ·65		− ·66	·49	− ·39	·41	·05	·18
·94	·90	− ·49	x	− ·27	·29	− ·28	− ·23	·47
·94	·89	− ·66		− ·16	·20	− ·23	− ·02	·06
− ·18	− ·16	·28	− ·27	x	− ·95	·94	− ·74	·51
− ·24	− ·06	·49	− ·16		− ·96	·96	− ·68	·53
·19	·19	− ·16	·29	− ·95	x	− ·99	·80	− ·40
·25	·08	− ·39	·20	− ·96		− ·995	·78	− ·52
− ·14	− ·15	·06	− ·28	·94	− ·99	x	− ·79	·34
− ·29	− ·13	·41	− ·23	·96	− ·995		− ·80	·52
− ·31	− ·28	·01	− ·23	− ·74	·80	− ·79	x	− ·69
·09	·08	·05	− ·02	− ·68	·78	− ·80		− ·48
·48	·50	·15	·47	·51	− ·40	·34	− ·69	x
− ·07	− ·02	·18	·06	·53	− ·52	·52	− ·48	

(in italics) the results obtained for Class B.

When we turn to the analyses of the individual cases, discussed in the following chapters, the picture we get is completely different. The relationships between behaviour variables are found to differ from case to case. It is therefore quite illegitimate to assume that aggregated population data can be used to obtain information on individual behaviour dynamics.

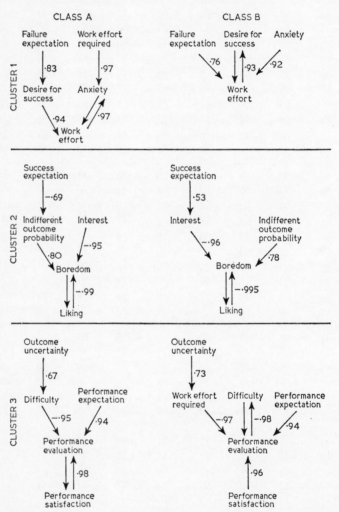

FIGURE 11 MCQUITTY LINKAGE STRUCTURE OF VARIABLES

At the same time, the properties of populations constitute a research topic in its own right both for its theoretical interest and for its practical implications. However, data analysis at this level presupposes the existence of models or theories of population properties which we do not as yet have.

In all the cases that will be discussed in later chapters, direct links exist between work effort, work effort required, and anxiety about examination results. The variable selected from the second cluster for case-study analysis is degree of boredom; and those from the third cluster are performance expectation and outcome uncertainty.

The major difficulty encountered in the quantitative analysis of individual cases is the very high degree of data reliability required. Any attempts at deception and counter-deception are certain to lead to useless results. Beyond this, the present method makes considerable demands on self-insight. Further, the method is very sensitive to error, since even a small number of errors will complicate the analysis and a large number of errors may make it quite impossible to interpret the results. In the present study about 10 per cent of cases were found to be suitable for analysis. At the same time, the analysis of each single case is still very time-consuming, so that it would have been impossible to carry out an analysis of more than a limited number of cases.

As far as the remainder of the cases are concerned, it should be possible to develop techniques for separating cases with a high proportion of unreliable data from cases where the relationships between behaviour variables are of a more complex type. With regard to the former, alternative techniques based on interviewing might provide better results.

At the present stage, therefore, the method should be used as a research technique whose chief advantage is that it produces results for a large number of cases in a minimum of time. A good deal more methodological work will need to be done before it can be used as a general diagnostic tool.

We shall finally need to consider to what extent the present technique satisfies the criteria that have to be met for carrying out quantitative case-study analysis, set out in Chapter 3. This will make it possible to identify possible sources of error that may arise.

Requirements

1a. The behavioural characteristics of school subjects are each specifiable by a single measure, so that the situation existing with respect to each task unit has the characteristics of a simple behaviour system.

1b. All measures have been formulated with respect to the same task units.

2a. Possible time units might be a quarter-year ending with an intermediate examination, or the total academic year. Both time-periods appear too long to obtain stable measures. Instead, pupils were asked to use the 'just now', that is, the subjective present as the time basis for measurement.

2b. All measures were obtained simultaneously. An additional requirement is that each pupil does in fact use the same time basis throughout.

3. All measures were based on the pupils' perception of the situation, and are thus based on the same frame of reference throughout.

4. A set of six variables will be used for functional network analysis. A set of four basic equations has to be formulated in each case, which can be tested by means of sixteen derivable equations.

5. The crucial requirement for the cross-sectional case-study technique is that, for each pupil, the situational structure with respect to each school subject has the same dynamic properties. Specifically, for each pupil the parameters of the behaviour network have to be identical for each school subject, so that the measures obtained for each task can be treated as different possible states of the same system.

CHAPTER 8

Behavioural Worlds

Work Effort and Emotional Response
under Conditions of Outcome Uncertainty

———————◆———————

SUMMARY

This chapter presents the case-study evidence which shows that principles of behaviour can vary from person to person. These findings cannot be accounted for in terms of traditional behaviour theories.

In the application of the basic postulates of generalized behaviour theory, a projective dimensional technique is introduced which makes it possible to derive each of the relationships found between work effort, work effort judged to be required, anxiety about the outcome, and boredom experienced, given that these variables are directly linked in the behaviour network.

———————◆———————

WORK EFFORT UNDER CONDITIONS OF OUTCOME UNCERTAINTY

The correlation analyses of the data from two school classes showed consistently that work effort expended on different school subjects increases with the work effort judged to be required ($r = \cdot93$ and $\cdot83$) and increases with the anxiety about examination results ($r = \cdot97$ and $\cdot92$).

If, however, the relationships between these variables are plotted for each pupil separately, a different kind of relationship is found in almost every case.

Figure 12 shows the results obtained for cases where it can be shown or inferred that work effort, work effort required, and anxiety are directly linked in the behaviour network.

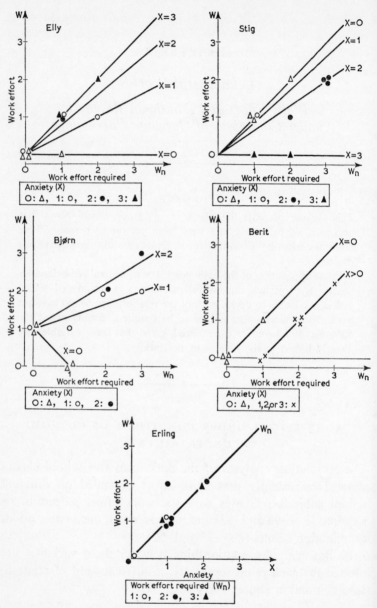

FIGURE 12 PRINCIPLE 1: WORK EFFORT AS A FUNCTION OF WORK EFFORT JUDGED TO BE REQUIRED AND OF ANXIETY ABOUT EXAMINATION RESULTS

Let us start with the relationship obtained for Elly. Here, in fact, work effort increases both with work effort required and with anxiety. If there is no anxiety, no work effort is made, and only if anxiety increases to a maximum does work effort correspond to work effort required.

Now suppose Elly's relationship is shifted upwards, then we arrive at the results obtained for Bjørn. Here, if there is no anxiety, work effort decreases with work effort required.

Stig's results show the same type of multiplicative relationship as those of Elly, but the effect of anxiety is reversed. Instead of stimulating effort, anxiety inhibits effort. Only when anxiety is absent will work effort correspond to work effort required. As anxiety increases to a maximum, work effort becomes completely inhibited.

In the case of Berit, anxiety has an all-or-none effect. If there is no anxiety, work effort made corresponds to work effort required; however, in the presence of anxiety, whatever the amount, a uniform decrease in work effort occurs.

A possible response to the situation might be to let work effort simply correspond to the amount of work judged to be required. Greater or lesser anxiety about examination results might be experienced, but this would have no effect on work effort. The person would in this case be immune to behavioural manipulation by means of anxiety induction. No case of this type was found.

Two cases were found, however, of which Erling is one, where work effort depended simply on the degree of anxiety experienced quite independent of the amount of work judged to be required.

Although the relationships obtained are noticeably diverse, inspection of the results does show a number of invariant characteristics. To begin with, the relationship between work effort (W) and work effort judged to be required (W_n), where this exists, is consistently of a linear form when anxiety is kept constant. (Prediction on a quantal scale requires that theoretical values diverge less than $\pm \frac{1}{2}$ of a scale unit.) Further, in five of the cases examined, a condition exists where $W = W_n$.

This shows that work effort and work effort judged to be required have the same dimension.

The relationship of anxiety to work effort and work effort required is

(a) monotonic and asymptotic, or
(b) linear, or
(c) all or none, which means that the function can take the value of only zero or unity.

Each of these relationships is a special case of a projective or bilinear function.

We shall in the following apply the postulates to demonstrate that, if the three variables are directly linked in the behaviour network, the functional relationship can take only one form, and each of the relationships shown in *Figure 12* turns out to be a special case of this function. We shall then go on to derive the possible larger networks which include boredom as a variable.

It should be noted that the validity of a given theoretical equation can rarely be tested by a single data plot, but requires systematic testing within a larger network of behaviour variables.

According to the two basic postulates discussed in Chapter 3:

All variables that refer to the internal state of a simple behaviour system can be defined in terms of the dimension [P]. Variables of dimension [P] are subject to linear scale-transformations.

Work effort (W) has already in Chapter 6 been shown to be an internal variable of dimension [P]. Work effort judged to be required (W_n) refers to the possibility that the person has of controlling the performance outcome by means of his own effort, which suggests that it is an internal variable. Since a condition exists where $W = W_n$, that is, work effort is equal to work effort judged to be required, both variables must have the same dimension.[1]

[1] If work effort requirements were based on personal demands rather than on task requirements, then the variable would be transactional.

It will be convenient to write the linear scale-transformation:

$$\pi(W) = \alpha_1 W + \alpha_2$$

All variables that refer to the transactional state of a simple behaviour system can be defined in terms of the dimension [S]. Variables of dimension [S] are subject to projective scale-transformations.

Anxiety (X) has to be defined simultaneously in terms of the state of the person and the expected state of the environment, and is therefore a transactional-type variable. We write the projective scale-transformation:

$$\rho(X) = \frac{\beta_1 X + \beta_2}{\beta_3 X + \beta_4}$$

Since this is a ratio of two linear transformations, it is sometimes also referred to as a bilinear transformation. This function will normally approach a limiting value. However, if $\beta_3 = 0$, and say $\beta_4 = 1$, then we obtain a linear form

$$\beta_1 X + \beta_2$$

and suppose $\beta_2 = 0$, $\beta_1 = \beta_3 = 1$, and let β_4 become an infinitestimally small variable which we shall denote by $\beta_4 = \varepsilon$, then we obtain

$$\frac{X}{X + \varepsilon}$$

an all-or-none function which is zero when X is zero, and unity for all other values of X.

These are, in fact, the three types of relationship between anxiety and the work effort variables that were found in the results shown in *Figure 12*.

We shall now introduce the method of *projective dimensional analysis*, which provides a very simple technique for deriving the total set of theoretically possible relationships between behaviour variables. The method is best explained by means of an actual example.

PRINCIPLE 1

THE RELATIONSHIP OF WORK EFFORT, WORK EFFORT REQUIRED, AND ANXIETY

Anxiety (X) as a transactional variable has the dimension $[S]$ and enters into relationships in the projective form

$$\rho(X) = \frac{\beta_1 X + s_1}{\beta_2 X + s_2} = \frac{[S]}{[S]} = [1]$$

The additive parameters s_1 and s_2 have in this case the dimension $[S]$, and β_1, β_2 are dimensionless parameters. The anxiety variable is therefore already in a dimensionless form.

Quite generally:

1. Variables in a projective form are dimensionless.
2. Addition of a constant, multiplication by a constant, or inversion leaves the functional form of a projective expression unchanged.

Work effort (W) and work effort required (W_n) both have the dimension $[P]$ and enter into relationships with other behaviour variables in a linear form. We can in this case produce non-dimensional forms by dividing one variable by the other.[1]

A simpler method, which, moreover, generates the total set of possible relationships, results if instead we define a projective function in two variables:

$$\rho(W, W_n) = \frac{\alpha_1 W + \alpha_2 W_n + p_1}{\alpha_3 W + \alpha_4 W_n + p_2} = \frac{[P]}{[P]} = [1]$$

The additive parameters p_1, p_2 have the dimension $[P]$, and $\alpha_1, \alpha_2, \alpha_3, \alpha_4$ are dimensionless parameters. The projective function is therefore dimensionless. Further, this function is likewise unaffected by the addition of a constant, by multiplication by

---

[1] This method was used in Chapter 6 for deriving principles of behaviour under conditions of outcome predictability. There the aim was to derive a more limited number of relationships consistent with task constraints.

a constant, or by inversion. The relationship between the three variables can therefore take only the form

$$\rho(W, W_n) = f[\rho(X)]$$

According to Postulate 3 discussed in Chapter 6:

If the three variables are directly linked to one another, then the functional relationship f ( ) takes the form of a non-dimensional constant.

Since multiplication by a constant does not alter the form of a projective function, the generalized principle giving the relationship between work effort, work effort judged to be required, and anxiety is therefore

$$\rho(W, W_n) = \rho(X) \qquad \qquad \ldots \ldots (1)$$

which, written out in full, is

$$\frac{\alpha_1 W + \alpha_2 W_n + p_1}{\alpha_3 W + \alpha_4 W_n + p_2} = \frac{\beta_1 X + s_1}{\beta_2 X + s_2}$$

Provided that the three variables are directly linked to one another, the relationship can take only this form.

Inversion of the expression on either side of the equation, or addition or multiplication by a constant, can produce no change in the form of the equation. The results shown in *Figure 12* can now be derived as special cases of this function.

For the purpose of deriving special cases it will be convenient to write the principle in the form

$$\frac{\pi_1(W) + \pi_3(W_n)}{\pi_2(W) + \pi_4(W_n)} = \frac{\pi_5(X)}{\pi_6(X)}$$

where $\pi(W)$ denotes a linear transformation of W which can take the form $\alpha W + \beta$, αW, W, β, 1, 0, depending on the values taken by α and β.

Table 9 shows how each of the relationships in *Figure 12* is derivable as a special case of the generalized equation, by choosing appropriate terms for each of the linear forms.

TABLE 9 LINEAR COMPONENTS OF THE GENERALIZED BEHAVIOUR PRINCIPLE 1

Linear components	Elly	Bjørn	Stig	Berit	Erling
$\pi_1(W)$	W	$W - a_4$	W	W	W
$\pi_2(W)$	0	0	0	0	0
$\pi_3(W_n)$	0	0	0	$-W_n$	0
$\pi_4(W_n)$	W_n	W_n	W_n	1	1
$\pi_5(X)$	$a_1 X$	$a_1(X - a_3)$	$a_2(a_3 - X)$	$-X$	X
$\pi_6(X)$	$X + a_2$	$X + a_2$	$a_3(a_2 - X)$	$X + \epsilon$	1

The linear components generate the specific principle that operates in the behavioural universe of each pupil.

The equations obtained, together with the parameters used for fitting, are as follows:

Elly
$$W = a_1 W_n \frac{X}{X + a_2}$$
$$a_1 = 2, \ a_2 = 3$$

Bjørn
$$W = a_1 W_n \frac{X - a_3}{X + a_2} + a_4$$
$$a_1 = a_4 = 1, \ a_2 = a_3 = \tfrac{1}{2}$$

Stig
$$W = \frac{a_2}{a_3} W_n \frac{a_3 - X}{a_2 - X}$$
$$a_2 = 4, \ a_3 = 3$$

Berit
$$W = W_n - \frac{X}{X + \varepsilon}$$

(ε is an infinitesimally small value. The equation requires no parameters for fitting.)

Erling
$$W = X$$

The special characteristics of each relationship can be examined by considering the conditions under which work effort made equals work effort required ($W = W_n$) and the conditions under which no work effort is made (*Table 10*).

TABLE 10 CONDITIONS UNDER WHICH WORK EFFORT MADE EQUALS WORK EFFORT REQUIRED, AND UNDER WHICH NO WORK EFFORT IS MADE

	Conditions under which:	
	Work effort is equal to work effort required	*No work effort is made*
Elly	If there is extreme anxiety ($X = 3$)	Either if there is no anxiety or if no work effort is required
Bjørn	None—note that work effort can exceed the effort required to do well in the subject	Only if there is no anxiety
Stig	If there is no anxiety	Either if there is extreme anxiety ($X = 3$) or if no work effort is required
Berit	If there is no anxiety	If no work effort or little work effort is required, but anxiety is experienced
Erling	None—work effort is not related to work effort required	If there is no anxiety

Except for the very simplest cases, the formulation and fitting of single functional relationships should generally be avoided. A test of the validity of a given functional relationship and possible parametric values requires a test of the derivations obtained within a larger network of behaviour variables.

In so far as all variables are measured on a quantal intensity scale which can take only integral values, fitted values are restricted to integral values. In most cases, the parametric values are easily obtained by examining the conditions under which work effort equals work effort required ($W = W_n$) and the conditions for no work effort ($W = 0$).

The network of relationships including boredom as an additional variable will now be investigated for Elly, Berit, and Bjørn.

PRINCIPLE 2

THE RELATIONSHIP OF BOREDOM, WORK EFFORT, AND WORK EFFORT REQUIRED

All three variables including boredom (B) have the dimension $[P]$. We can form three dimensionless projective ratios

$$\rho(W,W_n), \quad \rho(W_n,B), \quad \text{and} \quad \rho(W,B)$$

and obtain in this case three possible relationships

$$\rho(W,W_n) = \rho(W_n,B) \qquad \text{......(i)}$$

$$\rho(W,W_n) = \rho(W,B) \qquad \text{......(ii)}$$

$$\rho(W_n,B) = \rho(W,B) \qquad \text{......(iii)}$$

The equation for Elly is a special case of (i) and has the form

$$B - b_1 = b_2 W_n - \frac{b_3 W}{W_n} \qquad \text{......(2a)}$$

b_2, $b_3 > 0$ are non-dimensional parameters and $b_1 > 0$ has the dimension $[P]$ (see *Figure 13*).

Boredom in this case increases with the perceived work effort required but decreases with work effort.

The equation for Berit is a special case of (ii) and has the form

$$B = b_1 - \frac{W}{b_2}\left(1 + \frac{b_3}{W_n}\right) \qquad \text{......(2b)}$$

The relationship is similar in direction to that for Elly. Here, however, if some work effort is required and no work is carried out, then boredom has a constant value $B = b_1$. If no work effort is required and no work is carried out, then $B = b_1 - 0/0$, which means that the outcome with respect to boredom experienced is unpredictable (*Figure 14*).

The equation for Bjørn, which is a special case of (i), is more conveniently put in the form

$$W = a_1 W_n \left(1 - \frac{b_1}{b_2 W_n - B + b_3} \right) + a_4 \qquad \ldots\ldots(2c)$$

Work effort decreases with boredom. With boredom kept constant, an increase in work effort required initially decreases work effort and then increases it (*Figure 15*).

We can now go on to construct the total functional network of behaviour variables for Elly, Berit, and Bjørn.

BEHAVIOURAL NETWORKS

The Case of Elly

All the relationships for Elly shown in *Figures 12* and *13* are found to be monotonic. It was therefore possible to carry out a linear network analysis. The result, discussed in Chapter 4, showed that the cyclic order of variables is $W\ X\ B\ W_n$.

The network can be specified by any set of two basic principles, the remaining two principles being derivable.[1] For the purpose of quantitative formulation, principles 1 and 2 give the set of basic principles.

The network, in the case of Elly, is thus completely specified by:

1a. Work effort increases with work effort required and/or anxiety.

2a. Boredom increases with work effort required and/or decreases with work effort.

Given the above cyclic order of variables we obtain the two derived principles:

Ia. Boredom increases with work effort required and/or decreases with anxiety.

IIa. Boredom increases with work effort and/or decreases with anxiety.

[1] In a cyclic four-variable network every set of three variables will appear as directly linked. Postulate 3 can in this case be applied as a hypothesis to test whether for any given set of three variables a direct link exists.

The latter implies that work effort increases as a joint function of boredom and anxiety. However, as the linear network analysis showed, boredom does not increase work effort directly. The relationship is mediated by the work effort required. What would normally happen is that an increase in work required would increase work effort and at the same time increase the degree of boredom experienced.

Elly, it appears, functions best under conditions of anxiety,

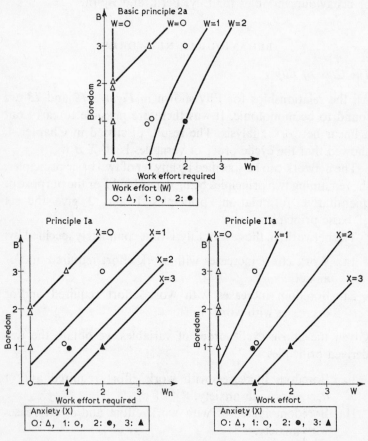

FIGURE 13 THE CASE OF ELLY: BOREDOM AS A FUNCTION OF WORK EFFORT AND WORK EFFORT JUDGED TO BE REQUIRED, AND DERIVED RELATIONSHIPS

which in her case has a direct stimulating effect on work effort and reduces boredom due to work load.

The complete network of functional relationships for Elly, derivable from the two basic principles in their quantitative form, is as follows:

basic principles

$$W = a_1 W_n \frac{X}{X+a_2} \qquad \text{......(1a)}$$

$$B - b_1 = b_2 W_n - \frac{b_3 W}{W_n} \qquad \text{......(2a)}$$

derived principles

$$B - b_1 = b_2 W_n - \frac{a_1 b_3 X}{X+a_2} \qquad \text{......(Ia)}$$

$$B - b_1 = \frac{b_2 W(X+a_2)}{a_1 X} - \frac{a_1 b_3 X}{X+a_2} \qquad \text{......(IIa)}$$

The network parameter values for the fitted equations are

$$b_2 = 1, \quad a_1 = b_1 = 2, \quad a_2 = b_3 = 3$$

A method that has been found to be useful in fitting the network of equations is to choose one data point as an anchorage point. A data point, preferably with extreme values on all variables, is chosen. In the present case the results obtained for English were chosen. One parameter value in Equations 1 and 2 is then used to obtain a perfect prediction for the variables associated with this subject. We exchange in this way one data point for two parameter values. The net result is that an estimate of only three parameters is now required to fit the total set of four equations. Another advantage is that an immediate check can be maintained on all computations.

The Case of Berit

All the relationships for Berit shown in *Figures 12* and *14* are monotonic. The linear network analysis in Chapter 4 (*Figure 6*) showed that the cyclic order of variables is W W_n X B.

The network can be completely specified by the two basic principles:

1b. Work effort increases with work effort required and/or decreases with anxiety experienced.

2b. Boredom increases with work effort required and/or decreases with work effort.

With the given cyclic order of variables we obtain the two derived principles:

Ib. Boredom increases with anxiety and/or decreases with work effort required.

IIb. Boredom decreases with work effort and/or increases with anxiety.

The latter implies that work effort increases on the one hand with anxiety experienced and decreases on the other hand with boredom.

Principle 2 is the only one that is qualitatively similar for Berit and Elly. However, the functional relationship is of a different type.

The network of functional relationships for Berit is:

basic principles

$$W = a_1 W_n - \frac{a_2 X}{X + a_3} \qquad \qquad \text{......(1b)}$$

$$B = b_1 - \frac{W}{b_2}\left(1 + \frac{b_3}{W_n}\right) \qquad \qquad \text{......(2b)}$$

derived principles

$$B = b_1 - \frac{a_1 b_3}{b_2} - \frac{a_1}{b_2} W_n + \frac{a_2}{b_2} \frac{X}{X + a_3}\left(1 + \frac{b_3}{W_n}\right) \qquad \text{......(Ib)}$$

$$B = b_1 - \frac{W}{b_2}\left(1 + \frac{a_1 b_3}{W + \left(\frac{a_2 X}{X + a_3}\right)}\right) \qquad \text{......(IIb)}$$

With the parameter values

$$a_1 = a_2 = 1, \quad b_1 = b_2 = 2, \quad b_3 = 3, \quad a_3 = \varepsilon$$

ε is defined as an infinitesimal small value. With $a_3 = \varepsilon$, anxiety has an all-or-none effect in all relationships.

Where all relationships are monotonic, linear network analysis constitutes a technique that not only is simple but provides information about the linkage of variables which is not easily inferred from functional relationship analysis. Networks of monotonic relationships are, however, quite rare.

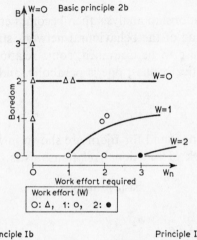

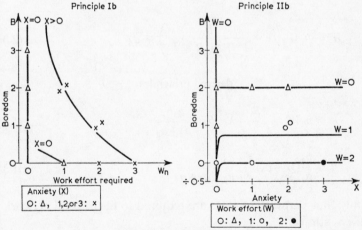

FIGURE 14 THE CASE OF BERIT: BOREDOM AS A FUNCTION OF WORK EFFORT AND WORK EFFORT JUDGED TO BE REQUIRED, AND DERIVED RELATIONSHIPS

This means that correlational analysis techniques are valid only in exceptional circumstances. In the majority of cases, relationships are non-monotonic, because

(i) either the direction of the relationship changes at critical values of the associated variable
(ii) or the relationship is of a parabolic or more complex form.

Functional relationship analysis then becomes essential to gain an understanding of the behavioural network structure.

In the last case to be examined, some relationships change direction at critical values, one is parabolic, and one is linear.

The Case of Bjørn

The relationships found for Bjørn are shown in *Figures 12* and *15*. The network of functional relationships is:

basic principles

$$W = a_1 W_n \frac{X - a_3}{X + a_2} + a_4 \qquad \dots\dots(1c)$$

$$W = a_1 W_n \left(1 - \frac{b_1}{b_2 W - B + b_3} \right) + a_4 \qquad \dots\dots(2c)$$

derived principles

$$B = b_2 W_n - \frac{b_1}{a_2 + a_3} X + b_3 - \frac{a_2 b_1}{a_2 + a_3} \qquad \dots\dots(\text{Ic})$$

$$B = \frac{b_2}{a_1} (W - a_4) \frac{X + a_2}{X - a_3} - \frac{b_1}{a_2 + a_3} X + b_3 - \frac{a_2 b_1}{a_2 + a_3} \qquad \dots\dots(\text{IIc})$$

Only four parameter values are required to fit the total network of equations

$$a_1 = a_4 = 1, \qquad a_2 = a_3 = \tfrac{1}{2}$$

$$b_1 = 2, \qquad b_2 = b_3 = \tfrac{3}{2}$$

It will be seen that

1c. Work effort increases with work effort required if anxiety is experienced, but decreases with work effort required if there is no anxiety,

2c. Work effort decreases with boredom (if $W_n > 0$). With boredom constant, work effort initially declines with work effort required ($B > 0$) and then increases.

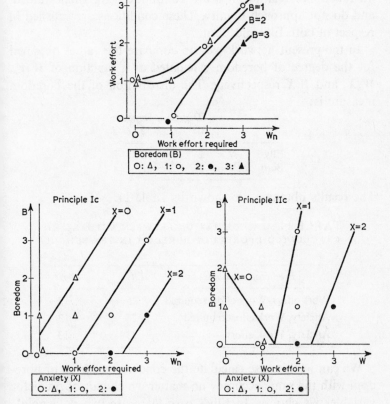

FIGURE 15 THE CASE OF BJØRN: BOREDOM AS A FUNCTION OF WORK EFFORT AND WORK EFFORT JUDGED TO BE REQUIRED, AND DERIVED RELATIONSHIPS

The derived relationships are:

Ic. Boredom increases with work effort required and/or decreases with anxiety.

IIc. Boredom increases with work effort if anxiety is high, but decreases with work effort if there is no anxiety.

We can finally test an implication from the first postulate, namely, that we should in principle be able to predict the value of any behaviour variable from any other two behaviour variables, given a simple behaviour system and parametric steady-state conditions. This can be the case, however, only if all functional relationships are continuous, are single-valued, and do not approach infinity. These conditions are satisfied in respect of both Elly and Berit.

In the present network we can compare the values obtained for the degree of boredom calculated as a function of WW_n, W_nX, and WX respectively. The distribution of the boredom measure is:

| | | *Degree of boredom* | | | |
		0	*1*	*2*	*3*
Elly	$N =$	2	4	2	2
Berit	$N =$	3	3	3	1

The results obtained are shown in Table 11.

TABLE 11 MEAN DEVIATION BETWEEN ACTUAL AND CALCULATED DEGREES OF BOREDOM IN TEN SCHOOL SUBJECTS

Predictor variables	Elly	Berit
Work effort, Work effort required	·25	·13
Anxiety, Work effort required	·24	·13
Anxiety, Work effort	·23	·13

We can in this case calculate the concurrent degree of boredom with the same accuracy no matter which pair of predictor variables we choose. In Elly's case there are two data points with a discrepancy of one scale unit. In Berit's case there is only one such data point.

CHAPTER 9

Outcome Uncertainty and Performance Expectation

————◆————

SUMMARY

This chapter continues the analysis of the case of Elly by the construction of the total network of relationships between outcome uncertainty, expected performance level, work effort, work effort required, boredom, and anxiety.

————◆————

PRINCIPLE 3

WORK EFFORT AS A FUNCTION OF WORK EFFORT REQUIRED AND OUTCOME UNCERTAINTY

Outcome uncertainty is measurable on a probability-type scale which runs from complete certainty ($U = 0$) to complete uncertainty ($U = 1$). Both values have to be looked at as ideal limiting points which are never reached in practice. Our chance of achieving a given future outcome may be ·9, ·99, or ·999 but can never reach 1·0. There will therefore be a critical probability value beyond which the outcome is responded to as being certain, and also a critical value beyond which the outcome is considered to be unpredictable and thus uncontrollable.

The uncertainty scale has in this case two critical points. One parametric point $U_0 > 0$ is the operative zero value of the scale. At this point the outcome is responded to as certain. $U_1 < 1$ is the operative maximum value. At this point the outcome is responded to as unpredictable.

These parameter values may vary quite widely. One person even under the most favourable conditions possible, say, a

·9999 chance in his favour, will still consider the fact that there is a ·0001 chance against him as sufficient to make the outcome less than completely certain. At the other extreme, the gambler, equally aware that complete randomness is never perfectly achieved, will accept even an infinitesimal bias from a near-perfect 50:50 outcome as a sufficient margin for possible exploitation in his favour.

Now, clearly, no work effort (W) will be deployed either if the outcome is perceived as completely certain or if it is perceived as being completely uncertain. Thus $W = 0$ either if $U = U_0$ or if $U = U_1$. In between these values, some degree of work effort will be deployed.

In this case

$$W = f\left[(U - U_0)(U_1 - U)\right]$$

The relationship will have a parabolic form.

Outcome variance can be separated into two components:

(i) Outcome variance which can be controlled and thus neutralized by means of work effort.
(ii) Outcome variance which is not under the person's control.

That portion of the outcome variance which is considered to be controllable corresponds to the work effort judged to be required to achieve a satisfactory outcome (W_n), and the remainder is that which is perceived as uncontrollable outcome uncertainty.

It follows that outcome uncertainty has the same dimension as work effort. This is all the information we require to write the dimensional equations. However, we can go a little further by means of conceptual analysis.

Work effort judged to be needed to achieve a satisfactory outcome on a given task corresponds to the effort that the person judges he can effectively apply to control the outcome variance.

If U_1 is low, then only a low level of uncertainty will be responded to as being controllable by means of work effort. We may say in this case that the person lacks confidence.

If U_1 is high, then a high level of uncertainty will be judged to be controllable by means of work effort. But this means that the maximal uncertainty looked at as a task-dependent variable corresponds to the amount of work effort judged to be required to achieve a satisfactory performance level (W_n), so that we can write

$$U_1 = \alpha W_n + \beta$$

and, by substituting in the above equation,

$$W = f\left[(U - U_0)(\alpha W_n + \beta - U)\right]$$

We can now proceed to the formulation of the principle by means of dimensional analysis.

Outcome uncertainty (U), work effort (W), and work effort required (W_n) are all of the same dimension [P]. Just as in the case of the second principle, we obtain three dimensional equations:

$$\rho(U,W) = \rho(U,W_n) \qquad \qquad \text{......(3i)}$$

$$\rho(U,W) = \rho(W,W_n) \qquad \qquad \text{......(3ii)}$$

$$\rho(U,W_n) = \rho(W,W_n) \qquad \qquad \text{......(3iii)}$$

Of these, only the first equation is consistent with the condition that outcome uncertainty has two critical points, and, by writing the dimensional equation (3i) out in full, we obtain the third principle in the form

$$\frac{\alpha_1 W + \alpha_2 U + \alpha_3}{\alpha_4 W + \alpha_5 U + \alpha_6} = \frac{\beta_1 U + \beta_2 W_n + \beta_3}{\beta_4 U + \beta_5 W_n + \beta_6} \qquad \text{......(3)}$$

With α_2, α_3, α_4, $\beta_5 = 0$ and α_6, $\beta_1 < 0$ we arrive at the principle found in the case of Elly

$$W = \frac{d_1(U - U_0)(W_n - d_3 U + d_4)}{U + d_2} \qquad \text{......(3a)}$$

Work effort in this case is zero if the outcome is taken to be certain ($U = U_0$). As uncertainty increases, work effort first increases and then decreases until it reaches zero at the point where the amount of outcome uncertainty is responded to as uncontrollable by means of work effort. With the level of uncertainty constant, work effort increases at a linear rate with work effort judged to be required.

It will in the following be convenient to write

$$f(U,W_n) = \frac{d_1(U-U_0)}{U+d_2}(W_n - d_3U + d_4)$$

and

$$f(U,X) = \frac{d_1(U-U_0)(d_4 - d_3U)}{a_1(U+d_2)X - d_1(U-U_0)(X+a_2)}$$

The set of basic principles for Elly is in this case as follows:

basic principles

$$W = a_1 W_n \frac{X}{X+a_2} \qquad \ldots\ldots(1a)$$

$$B - b_1 = b_2 W - \frac{b_3 W}{W_n} \qquad \ldots\ldots(2a)$$

$$W = f(U,W_n) \qquad \ldots\ldots(3a)$$

from which we derive the total network of relationships between outcome uncertainty, work effort, work effort required, anxiety, and boredom:

derived principles

$$X = \frac{a_2 \cdot f(U,W_n)}{a_1 W_n - f(U,W_n)} \qquad \ldots\ldots(\text{IIIa})$$

$$W = a_1 X \cdot f(U,X) \qquad \ldots\ldots(\text{IVa})$$

$$B - b_1 = b_2 W_n - \frac{b_3 f(U,W_n)}{W_n} \qquad \ldots\ldots(\text{Va})$$

$$B - b_1 = b_2(X+a_2) \cdot f(U,X) - \frac{a_1 b_3 X}{X+a_2} \qquad \ldots\ldots(\text{VIa})$$

$$B - b_1 = b_2 \left[\frac{W(U+d_2)}{d_1(U-U_0)} + d_3U - d_4 \right] - \frac{b_3 W}{\dfrac{W(U+d_2)}{d_1(U-U_0)} + d_3U - d_4} \quad \ldots(\text{VIIa})$$

Figure 16 shows the fit obtained with the parameter values

$$d_1 = 3\cdot 2$$
$$U_0 = d_2 = \cdot 1$$
$$d_3 = 5, \quad d_4 = 1\cdot 2$$

All relationships with outcome uncertainty are found to have a parabolic shape.

Anxiety and work effort have very similar relationships to outcome uncertainty. If the outcome appears certain ($U = \cdot 1$), then no anxiety is experienced and no work effort is made. Principle IIIa shows that anxiety reaches a maximum value when potential outcome control is a maximum, that is, when the work effort that can be effectively applied to control the outcome is large relative to outcome uncertainty. It is here, where Elly perceives the outcome to be most highly dependent on her own skill and effort, that maximum anxiety is experienced, and also minimum boredom.

Now, the greater the work effort judged to be required by the task, the greater the degree of outcome uncertainty that can be successfully coped with. However, as uncertainty begins to swamp the effort that can be effectively applied, when

$$W_n = d_3 U - d_4 \text{ and thus } f(U, W_n) = 0,$$

anxiety disappears, and instead maximum boredom is experienced.

We may summarize, then, by saying that in the case of Elly:

(i) If the outcome is judged to be certain, no work effort is deployed and no anxiety is experienced.

(ii) To the extent that the outcome is perceived to be highly dependent on Elly's own effort and skill, rather than on extraneous factors, that is

$$W_n > d_3 U - d_4,$$

then maximum anxiety is experienced, there is little boredom, and work effort is a maximum.

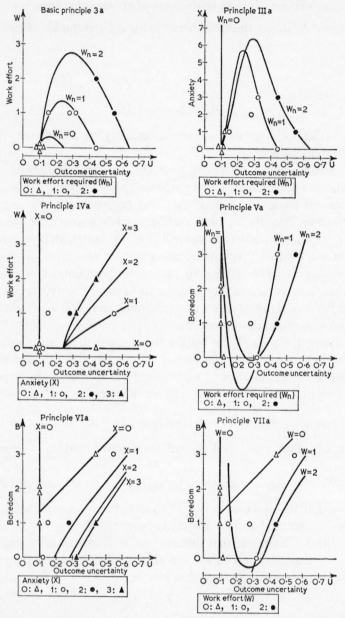

FIGURE 16 THE CASE OF ELLY: WORK EFFORT AS A FUNCTION OF WORK EFFORT JUDGED TO BE REQUIRED AND OF OUTCOME UNCERTAINTY, AND DERIVED RELATIONSHIPS

(iii) At the point when situational uncertainty cancels out the work effort that can be effectively applied, so that the outcome goes beyond possible control, anxiety disappears, no work effort is deployed, and maximum boredom with the task is experienced.

The relationships of boredom to uncertainty are found to be the reverse of those of work effort and anxiety. If the outcome is certain then the degree of boredom is not predictable. Boredom reaches a minimum for intermediate levels of uncertainty where a high degree of work effort is deployed and a high level of anxiety is experienced. From here on, boredom increases as outcome uncertainty increases and little or no work effort is deployed.

PRINCIPLE 4

PERFORMANCE EXPECTATION AS A FUNCTION OF BOREDOM AND ANXIETY

No direct relationship exists between the amount of work effort and skill applied to school work and the performance level in the form of examination grades that will finally be received. Apart from unpredictable personal factors such as the emotional state of the pupil at the time of the examination, there are a number of relevant external conditions which are not predictable. The pupil will not be given information about the examination questions. The evaluative criteria that will be employed are not explicit, nor are they constant—they may vary from year to year owing to policy decisions or to personal judgements made by whoever constructs and marks the examination papers.

The behaviour of a pupil cannot, in this situation, be related to the performance level that he will achieve, but it can be related to the performance level he expects to achieve.

The expected performance level is a transactional variable which depends both on the pupil's judgement of his performance capacity and on his judgement of the environmental conditions he is likely to encounter.

We shall, to begin with, construct the dimensional equation for the relationship between the expected performance level (P_e), which as a transactional variable of dimension [S] will be subject to a projective scale-transformation, and the work effort judged to be required (W_n) and the degree of boredom (B), both of which are internal variables of dimension [P]. Since only two dimensionless ratios can in this case be constructed, then, provided the three variables are directly linked, the equation can take only the form

$$\rho(P_e) = \rho(B, W_n)$$

which, written out in full, is

$$\frac{\delta_1 P_e + \delta_2}{\delta_3 P_e + \delta_4} = \frac{\gamma_1 B + \gamma_2 W_n + \gamma_3}{\gamma_4 B + \gamma_5 W_n + \gamma_6}$$

With the parametric conditions

$$\gamma_2, \ \gamma_3, \ \gamma_4 = 0, \qquad \delta_1, \ \delta_4, \ \gamma_5 < 0$$

we arrive at the principle found in the case of Elly, which has the form

$$B = b_2(m - W_n)\frac{P_1 - P_e}{P_e - P_0}$$

The equation has two critical parameters:

P_0 is the neutral point of the performance scale. In the case of Elly this corresponds to a C (satisfactory) grade. Below and above this point, most relationships to work effort and emotional response variables are reversed.

P_1 is the minimum expected performance level for any school subject. For Elly this value lies at the midpoint between the C and B grades.

In the following it will be convenient to choose as a basic principle one of the derived equations. This is the relationship of performance expectation to boredom and anxiety experienced, which can be derived with the help of Principle Ia

$$B = c_1(P_1 - P_e)\frac{c_2 - X}{X + a_2} \qquad \qquad ......(4a)$$

where $c_2 > X$.

According to Principle 4a, boredom decreases at a linear rate with expected performance level (anxiety kept constant). Boredom also decreases with anxiety experienced (expected performance level kept constant). In either case, boredom disappears when performance level reaches the maximum expected performance level P_1. This is one of the few relationships that are found to have a similar form in quite a large number of cases.

The fact that this triad of variables, including expected performance level, has the simplest functional form indicates that these three variables are directly linked to one another.

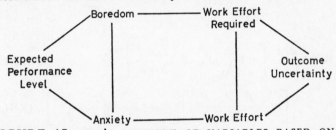

FIGURE 17 ELLY'S NETWORK OF VARIABLES BASED ON PRINCIPLES 1–4

We arrive in this case at Elly's total network of variables, shown in *Figure 17*. Outcome uncertainty is found to be a relatively objective judgement linked to work effort variables. Expected performance level is, on the other hand, linked to emotional response variables and thus is relatively more subjective. Since outcome uncertainty and expected performance level are the most distant pair of variables in the network, their relationship would be expected to be the most complex one. This is in fact the case.

The set of basic principles is as follows:

basic principles

$$W = a_1 W_n \frac{X}{X+a_2} \qquad \text{......(1a)}$$

$$B - b_1 = b_2 W - \frac{b_3 W}{W_n} \qquad \text{......(2a)}$$

$$B = c_1 (P_1 - P_e) \frac{c_2 - X}{X + a_2} \qquad \text{......(4a)}$$

from which we derive the total network of relationships between expected performance level, work effort, work effort required, anxiety, and boredom:

derived principles

$$B = b_2(m - W_n)\frac{P_1 - P_e}{P_e - P_0} \qquad \qquad \text{......(VIIIa)}$$

$$W = \frac{a_1 W_n}{a_2 + c_2}\left[c_2 - \frac{a_2 b_2}{c_1}\frac{(m - W_n)}{(P_e - P_0)}\right] \qquad \text{......(IXa)}$$

$$P_e - P_0 = \frac{b_2}{c_1}(m - W_n)\frac{X + a_2}{c_2 - X} \qquad \qquad \text{......(Xa)}$$

$$W = \frac{a_1 X}{X + a_2}\left[m + \frac{c_1}{b_2}(P_0 - P_e)\frac{c_2 - X}{X + a_2}\right] \qquad \text{......(XIa)}$$

$$W = \frac{1}{b_3}\left[m - \frac{B}{b_2}\left(\frac{P_e - P_0}{P_1 - P_e}\right)\right]\left[b_2 m + b_1 - B\left(\frac{P_1 - P_0}{P_1 - P_e}\right)\right]\text{...(XIIIa)}$$

where
$$c_1 > 0, \quad P_1 > P_0 > 0$$
$$c_2 > X, \quad P_1 \geqslant P_e$$

together with the following parametric equations

$$P_0 = P_1 - \frac{a_1 a_2 b_3}{c_1(a_2 + c_2)} \qquad \qquad \text{......(i)}$$

$$m = \frac{1}{b_2}\left(a_1 b_3 - b_1 - \frac{a_1 a_2 b_3}{a_2 + c_2}\right) \qquad \text{......(ii)}$$

The neutral and the maximum expected performance levels are found to be interdependent values.

The parameters for the two basic principles 1a and 2a have already been estimated in Chapter 8. Only three additional parameters are required to fit the total network of relationships. The derived principles are shown in *Figure 18*, with the estimated parameter values

$$c_1 = 3\cdot88, \quad c_2 = 4\cdot2, \quad P_1 = 3\cdot49$$

The derived values are

$$P_0 = 2\cdot845 \text{ and } m = 1\cdot5$$

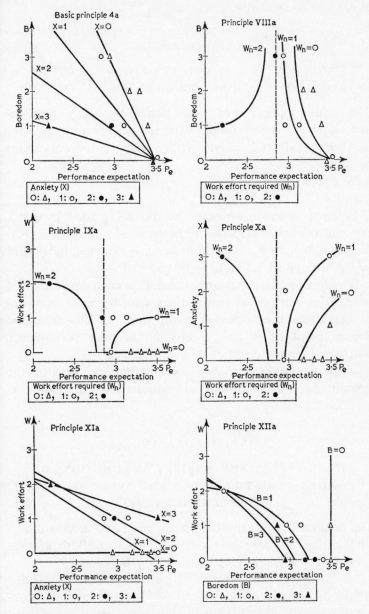

FIGURE 18 THE CASE OF ELLY: BOREDOM AS A FUNCTION OF
EXPECTED PERFORMANCE LEVEL AND OF ANXIETY, AND DE-
RIVED RELATIONSHIPS

PRINCIPLE VIIIa

BOREDOM AS A FUNCTION OF WORK EFFORT REQUIRED AND EXPECTED PERFORMANCE LEVEL

The relationship has three critical points: the neutral performance level P_0; the maximum expected performance level for any school subject P_1; and a critical value m for work effort required.

Whenever $P_e < P_0$ then $W_n > m$

and if $\quad P_e > P_0$ then $W_n < m$

In the present case, whenever less then a C grade is expected, very much work is perceived to be required to achieve a satisfactory outcome. If a C grade or better is expected, fairly hard or no work effort is judged to be required.

Boredom reaches a maximum value at the neutral performance level. With work effort required constant, boredom decreases to the extent that expected performance deviates from the neutral point either in the direction of poor performance outcome or in the direction of higher grades.

When the expected grade reaches its maximal level (in the present case for Norwegian and mathematics), no boredom is experienced.

PRINCIPLES IXA AND XA

WORK EFFORT AND ANXIETY AS FUNCTIONS OF WORK EFFORT REQUIRED AND EXPECTED PERFORMANCE LEVEL

The relationships obtained for work effort and anxiety are so similar that they are best discussed together. Both are the reverse of the relationship obtained for boredom.

No anxiety is experienced and no work effort is expended within the vicinity of the neutral performance level. Furthermore, no work effort is made and little anxiety is experienced if a chance of obtaining more than a C grade is perceived and no work effort is judged to be required to achieve this.

Both anxiety and work effort increase to a maximum the further the expected grade falls below the neutral point. Anxiety increases to a maximum, but work effort less so, the higher the potential grade that is judged to be achievable, provided that the outcome can be affected by means of work effort.

As in the previous findings on outcome uncertainty, there is a crucial distinction between those school subjects—such as religion, geography, and nature study—in which Elly perceives a chance of getting an acceptable grade without any special effort on her part, and those—such as foreign languages and mathematics—in which an acceptable grade cannot be achieved by her without a fair amount of work.

PRINCIPLE XIA

WORK EFFORT AS A FUNCTION OF ANXIETY AND EXPECTED PERFORMANCE LEVEL

Here, work effort and anxiety are found to have fundamentally different relationships with expected performance level.

Whereas anxiety *increases* with expected performance level (work effort kept constant), work effort *decreases* the higher the performance level expected, except when there is no anxiety and therefore no work effort.

PRINCIPLE XIIA

BOREDOM AS A FUNCTION OF WORK EFFORT AND EXPECTED PERFORMANCE LEVEL

With boredom kept constant, work effort decreases with performance level expected, except at the maximum expected performance level, when work effort expended becomes unpredictable.

The basic principle 4a is one of the few that have some degree of generality, at least to the extent that for quite a large number of persons it is found that boredom decreases jointly with anxiety and increasing performance expectation. In no case, however, does a specific functional relationship, or even any particular direction of relationships between behaviour variables, have universal validity. It appears, then, that the nearest we can come to in the way of a universal principle under conditions of outcome uncertainty relates to those cases where the dimensional equation can take only a single form.

Unlike behaviour based on determinate tasks, where reality constraints exist which limit the possible types of behavioural network that can emerge, no intrinsic constraints operate under conditions of outcome uncertainty, so that relationships can take almost any form and any direction within the limits set by the two basic postulates.

At the same time, some constraints may and presumably do operate within a given local culture. For instance, one of the most remarkable findings of the present study, both at the level of population analysis and at the level of individual cases, is the extent to which work effort depends on anxiety about examination results. This would appear to reflect one of the characteristics of the Norwegian educational system, which is that examination results almost exclusively determine the pupils' chances of educational advancement. Under these conditions, behaviour at school will more often be built around anxiety and boredom than around interest and the joy of discovery, and will be concerned more with the credits that can be earned by means of the task than with the task itself.

We started off with some very general principles for psychological theory construction and have ended up by producing, as one of our results, a basis for the development of diagnostic techniques. From the point of view of the historical logic of scientific development this is by no means surprising. In the history of the physical sciences each advance made in theory construction provided an essential basis for the development of measures of the specific characteristics of different materials.

However, there are important differences between the behavioural and the physical sciences. We are not able to compare different behavioural universes in terms of the absolute numerical values of variables or parameters. What we can do is to determine for each individual case the parametric structure, in terms of the relative size of parameters, and parameters that take zero values. It is this that determines the direction and shape of functional relationships, within the behaviour network structure, given the appropriate set of generalized behaviour principles.

It should be noted that algebraic methods are used throughout to arrive at qualitative structural information. If, in time, suitable non-numerical algebras based on projective geometry can be evolved, it will become possible to operate with non-numerical techniques. There are many possible directions of further development that it would seem worth while to explore. I am inclined, however, to believe that the best chance of further advancement in theory construction lies at the present stage in the further development of quantitative case-study techniques.[1]

---

[1] Reviewing all the individual behaviour principles derived and tested so far, and assuming the general validity of the projective dimensional technique, we may tentatively formulate the following universal law:

For any triad of behaviour variables which are directly linked to one another, the functional relationship corresponds to a projective transformation of a three-dimensional conic, excluding cyclic and elliptic functions.

PART THREE

Analysis of
Cognitive and Social Structures

CHAPTER 10

Interpersonal Life-space Analysis
A Code for Autobiographical Data
Obtained in Interviews

———◆———

SUMMARY

The life-space concept was introduced by Lewin about forty years ago in order to represent the situation that exists for a person as he perceives it. Revolutionary in its implications and pointing in the direction in which a behavioural science could be developed, it did not survive him. The main reason for this was that it could not develop beyond the stage of a conceptual framework without a method which would actually make it possible to map out and measure the life-space of a person. A number of frontal and tangential attacks on the problem (Herbst, 1952, 1954a, 1957a) led not to its solution but instead to the transformation of the life-space concept into the behaviour-system concept. I had by that time all but forgotten about the original problem until, in the course of a consultancy visit on a project concerned with the study of engaged couples, the question arose of working out a code for the available interview material. The data consisted of a series of interviews of both partners who talked about how they met, about their courtship, how they got engaged, the way in which their wedding arrangements were being made and, in later interviews, about their honeymoon and their early wedded life.[1]

———◆———

CONCEPTUAL FRAMEWORK

The life-space can be conceptually represented in terms of:

1. A set of cognitive elements
2. Relationships between elements
3. Affect associated with both elements and relations.

[1] The project was directed by Dr Rhona Rapoport at Harvard University School of Public Health (later at Harvard Medical School).

For the purpose of a first-level code which corresponds to a representation of the total situation at a first level of approximation, the elements of the life-space are defined as persons, who are:

1a. The self *I*, and other persons *O*, and
1b. A set of persons perceived as acting as a unit and referred to as 'we' (*IO*) in the case of self and other, or as 'they'.

At this stage, impersonal objects are treated not as independent elements but as attributes of persons. From a theoretical point of view, this means that every element of the life-space has itself a life-space of its own.

Relationships between elements, which, in this case, correspond to relationships between persons and perceived group units, are defined with respect to direction, which may be:

2a. From self to other, *I−O*
2b. From other to self, *O−I*
2c. Between other persons or groups.

Affect may be associated both with persons and with relationships between persons.

In the coding of affect, we distinguish between:

3a. Affect experienced by self, and
3b. Affect and feelings attributed by the interviewee to other persons who form part of his life-space.

Figure 19 shows the constituents of the life-space obtained from the code in diagrammatic form.

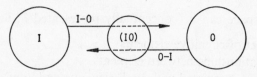

FIGURE 19 LIFE-SPACE REPRESENTATION FOR A TWO-PERSON SITUATION CONSISTING OF SELF (*I*), ANOTHER PERSON (*O*), AND WE (*IO*) COMPOSED OF SELF AND OTHER

INTERVIEW CODE

Persons are coded by capital letters:

The couple

  I The interviewee referring to himself or herself
  F The fiancé or fiancée.

Other Persons as a Class

  M Mothers
  P Fathers
  B Brothers
  S Sisters
  G Girl friends, female colleagues
  C Boy friends, male colleagues
  R Other relatives
  O Generalized others, somebody, or other persons, not sufficiently important to be specifically identified
  E Everybody, anybody, nobody.

Individuals

These are identified by suffixes to show whether they form part of the social network of the self or the fiancé(e). Persons are coded individually if a factual statement is made about them.

  M_i My mother lives near Boston.
  G_i My girl friend is a college student.
  M_f The fiancée's mother was not at home that day.
  B_f The fiancée's brother has a car.

A boy friend of both self and fiancé(e) is coded C_{if}.

Groups

Perceived group units referred to as 'we' or 'they' are coded in parentheses:

  (W) We, referring to self and fiancé(e).

147

In every other case, the persons forming part of the grouping are specifically identified:

(IC_i) 'We', referring to myself and my male friend.

(IM_i) 'We', referring to myself and my mother.

(FG_f) 'They', referring to the fiancée and the fiancée's girl friend.

In the case of parents, an identification suffix has to be added:

(M_iP_i) 'They', my parents.

(M_fP_f) 'They', the fiancé(e)'s parents.

(IM_iP_i) 'We', referring to myself and my parents.

(IO) 'We', people in my club, community, including myself.

If, however, the reference is to 'my brother and I', group perception cannot necessarily be inferred, and is coded as follows:

B_iI My brother and I took a taxi.

Personal Relationships

Personal relationships involve an actual or possible directed action between persons or groups. The relationship may be from self to other, from other to self, or between other persons or groups:

$I-F$ I went to see my fiancée. I disagreed with her (my fiancée) on this.

$F-I$ My fiancé asked me. He (my fiancé) wanted to take me out to the dog track.

Description of formal and kinship relations are coded as factual statements:

Elsa is my sister.	S_i
Ernie, he is my brother, talked this over with my father.	B_i-P_i

148

AFFECT

Affect may be associated with persons, with objects treated as attributes of persons, or with relationships. A distinction is made only between:

+ Positive affect

− Negative affect

Affect is coded only if it is clearly expressed and spontaneously communicated. Inference of covert affect is best left to the data-analysis stage.

In the research setting, it will be an advantage if the interviewer does not respond unduly to subtle and indirect communication even at the expense of appearing slightly stupid, in order to encourage explicit communication or the translation of more subtle communication into explicit terms for his benefit. Direct probing, if used as a last resort to force the expression of affect, has the tendency to draw what look to be or may be defensive replies. Replies of 'yes' or 'no' in answer to direct probing of affect fall under the heading of direct communication with the interviewer and may be disregarded or coded in square brackets to be analysed separately.

Frequently, feelings are vague and confused and the interviewee has to be left free to explore these by himself. Note, for instance, the following account given by the girl about her early meeting with her fiancé.

He asked me out/	$F-I$
and I said yes without hesitation/	$I-F$
so I must have liked him./	$I-F+$

It should be noted that affect is not coded until it is finally explicitly communicated.

Similarly:

I thought/	I
he would stop asking me out/	$F-I$
just to be frightful (to me)./	$F-I-$

Again, the attribution of negative affect is not coded until it is explicitly made.

Personal Affect

$I+$ I felt happy, I enjoyed this, I liked this.

No affect is coded for wanting or desiring something, unless the associated affect, which may be positive or negative, is clearly stated.

$I-$ I felt upset, annoyed, angry, worried, frightened, I did not like this.

A negative affect coding is given also for 'I did not want to do this' if no further explanation follows. However, if an explanation for not wanting is given which negates the implication of negative affect, such as 'I did not want to do something because I felt it was not a proper thing to do', or because 'I had already made other arrangements', negative affect should not be coded. Similarly, affect is not coded for factual reports such as being sick, going to the hospital, etc.

$W+$ We enjoyed this, we had a good time together.
$W-$ We did not get on well together, we had a fight about this.

Disagreeing about something as such is not coded for negative affect unless there is further evidence that negative feelings about the other were actually experienced.

Attributed Personal Affect

$F+$ The fiancée felt happy, she enjoyed herself at the dance.
$F-$ The fiancée was upset, she cried, she did not like the house.

Personal Relationship Affect

$I-M_i+$ I am very fond of my mother, I feel very close to her.

$I-G_i-$ I did not care much about this girl friend, I irritated my girl friend, I did not want to go out with her any more.

However, in the case of 'I did not want to go out with her that night', followed by an explanation which denies the affect, negative affect is not coded.

Affect is coded only if it is clearly implied and in all cases where 'I like you' or 'I dislike you' with reference to a specific relationship can be substituted without changing the meaning.

For instance:

This boy friend of mine asked me to go steady with him/	C_i-I+
but I did not want to (go steady with him)./	$I-C_i-$

However, in the following:

My fiancé asked me to marry him February 3rd/	$F-I$
and I got my hope chest (from him) February 4th./	$F-I$

This is a factual statement and no affect is coded.

Object Relationship Affect

Affect may be associated with a person or some part of a person, or with some object associated with a person. The suffix x is, in this case, used to code that the affect is directed towards an object which forms part of or is associated with the person. For instance:

She was wearing this, like a one-piece slacks outfit, it's got a zipper all the way down here,/	F
and I couldn't stand the outfit./	$I-F_x-$

I told my father/	$I-P_i$
why I saw the advantages of getting married in April/	I
before I went into the service,/	I

and he tried to discount every one I said;/	$P_i - I_x -$
and finally, I told him, well, what objections are there?/	$I - P_i$

Negative affect is scored not because the father said no, or disagreed about the date, but because no explanation was given, so that the son in this case perceived the father as not liking his idea.

Similarly, for affect experienced towards an object associated with or belonging to oneself:

$I_x +$ I like my apartment, my job.
$F_x +$ My fiancée is fond of her dress, her hair style.

My fiancée was wearing this one-piece slacks outfit,/	F
and I couldn't stand the outfit./	$I - F_x -$
She loves them,/	$F_x +$
but I couldn't stand it./	$I - F_x -$
But after that, I let her know/	$I - F$
that I didn't like it/	$I - F_x -$
and for her to throw it away./	F

Personal Evaluation

A distinction has to be made between the evaluation of a person in terms of his personal characteristics, and feelings experienced towards him. It is possible to ascribe positive characteristics to a person, such as that he is kind, gentle, or intelligent, but to dislike him, or to be in love with a person who is perceived as being cruel, ugly, or egotistical. If the personality organization is relatively undifferentiated, inconsistencies of this type are not easily maintained. Balance between evaluation and interpersonal affect can in this case be obtained by modulating the adjective kind to fussy, gentle to soft, intelligent to crafty, or by giving the term aggressive a desirable connotation as found, for instance, in American advertisements for salesmen.

$F + ve$ She (the fiancée) is attractive, she is a good cook.
$I - ve$ I am no good, stupid.

In every case the evaluative meaning of the description has to be judged in the total context.

Evaluation coding is used only if no relationship is specified. Otherwise relationship coding is applied:

I have never asked my fiancée to come up to my apartment,/	$I-F$
because I felt that it wasn't right./	I
About these other girls I just didn't care./	$I-G-$
Probably the biggest impression she made on me was that she to me,/	$F-I$
she was a very nice girl,/	$F+ve$
and that she had been brought up right./	$F+ve$

Conditional Affect

Reference to affect which might be or is expected to be experienced by oneself or others is coded in parentheses:

I was going to have a good time no matter what.	$I(+)$
Most girls wouldn't probably enjoy it at the dog track./	$G(-)$
I wanted to find out/	I
whether I liked my fiancée./	$I-F(+)$

Table 12 summarizes the affect categories in terms of self and fiancé(e).[1]

---

[1] The coding technique, which has emerged from a field theoretical framework, is conceptually related to the coding scheme developed by Mills (1952) for the analysis of group discussion data. The code is based on the location and direction of the communication content in terms of whether it is internal or external to the group, and in each case the content may be associated with positive, neutral, or negative affect. This code has been extended and applied by Mishler and Waxler (1964) to the analysis of individual members of family discussion groups. An objectivist method is employed, each act being coded as an isolated element. Affect is coded in terms of the assumed common cultural meaning and not in terms of the affective meaning implied by the context. For instance, to understand an idea, to play the piano, to strive, to be sensitive, are coded as implying positive states of people. The present code may presumably also be applicable to the analysis of group discussion data; however, the material would not seem to be suitable for life-space analysis. Another similar linguistic unit analysis has been used by Mehrabian (1966) to study the relationship of psychological distance between communicator and object to the explicit affect associated with the object.

TABLE 12 AFFECT AND EVALUATION CATEGORIES

With respect to:	Person	Part of a person, or object associated with a person
Affect experienced by self	$I^\pm$	$I_x{}^\pm$
Affected attributed to another person	$F^\pm$	$F_x{}^\pm$
Relationship affect	$I\text{-}F^\pm$	$I\text{-}F_x{}^\pm$
	$F\text{-}I^\pm$	$F\text{-}I_x{}^\pm$

Personal evaluation $I+ve, I-ve, F+ve, F-ve$

CODING CONVENTIONS

Repetitive Communication

Repetition of the same message in slightly different forms may be due to difficulties in adequately verbalizing one's perceptions and feelings, or due to concern that the message may be ambiguous or subject to distorted interpretation by the interviewer. The incidence of repetitive type of communication may thus provide a possible measure of the extent to which the person is concerned with minimizing distortion, at least where the content is relatively neutral or positive. Where the content is more negative, repetitive communication may be due to not wanting to accept one's experience or to unwillingness to convey it accurately. Repetition in this case would tend to be associated with anxiety.

In the case of sequential repetition, only a single code category is used. However, if the same content reappears at a later stage, it is coded again. For instance, in the example already discussed:

> Probably the biggest impression my fiancée
> made on me was that she to me . . . $F-I$

This is coded only once. The added 'she to me' is made to avoid the interviewer's interpreting the statement as a general evaluation when what the interviewee means to convey is that the following are his own personal feelings about his fiancée, and that somebody else, including the interviewer, may have a different impression of her.

My fiancée's mannerisms were just right and
I liked them very much. $\qquad I - F_x +$

Here the interviewee is quite aware of the affect coding problem we have previously discussed. The statement 'just right' might be interpreted by the interviewer to mean that positive affect was experienced, but it might also imply a detached factual judgement. By adding 'I liked them very much', the interviewee makes certain that the interviewer interprets the message correctly as implying positive affect.

Incomplete Communication

Over-elaboration is one characteristic found in verbal communication that is less prevalent in written documents, since, when writing, we tend to choose whichever of several phrases that present themselves seems to express best what we want to convey and is least open to distorted interpretation by the reader. Even more common, however, is the dropping out of content which, from previous information given, is judged to be self-evident and would be redundant if repeated again and again. The dropped-out content is nearly always supplied by the listener without his realizing that he is doing so. However, for coding purposes, the missing content has to be explicitly restituted.

For instance, the transcript referred to above reads in the original as follows (the content that is redundant from the point of view of communication in the context is added in parentheses):

He (my boy friend) wanted to go steady (with me)/
and I didn't (want to go steady with him).

In the interview setting, one of the tasks of the interviewer will be to spot incomplete or confused communication where the missing content cannot be supplied and to ask questions to clarify or check.

Passive Voice

Sentences expressed in the passive voice need to be put into the active form. For instance, 'She was invited by us' is read as 'We invited her'.

Interwoven Sentences

For coding purposes, the references have to be disentangled. For instance, 'My brother took the papers for me to my father' states that

My brother did something for me/	$B_i - I$
by taking the papers to my father./	$B_i - P_i$

Meta-communication

These are remarks about the communication itself, which have to be excluded from the interview content analysis, but may be analysed separately (Mishler and Waxler, 1964). The code category is in this case put in parentheses. For instance:

[I]   I think what actually happened was . . .
      What I mean is . . .
      I think it got to a point where . . .
      I don't remember exactly what happened next.

If, however, the thinking, guessing, expecting, etc. form part of the account itself, they are taken to form part of the situation described and are coded as a normal self-reference: For instance:

I think/	I
my fiancé did this/	F
because he felt upset./	$F -$

One way of testing whether a given phrase should be coded as meta-communication or not is to transpose it into the past tense and see how this affects the meaning of the sentence. In the above sentence, transposition into the past gives:

I thought my fiancé did this because he felt upset

which does not basically change the meaning of the sentence. However, if 'I think I met her brother' is transposed into the past, 'I thought I was meeting her brother', a completely different meaning results and the 'I think' is coded as meta-communication.

Direct communications to the interviewee's partner in a joint interview are similarly coded in parentheses:

$[I - F]$ Addressing the fiancé(e):

            Do you remember what happened?
            How did you feel about this?

For instance:

My fiancé felt/	F
the same way I did, that going steady was something serious,/	I
didn't you?/	$[I - F]$

Communication to the interviewer, such as 'I am not quite sure what you mean', may be either disregarded or coded in parentheses in the same way.

Secondary Communication

The interview content may refer not only to the life-space of the person but also to the life-space of others. The code already accommodates affect said to be experienced by, and perceptions of, others. However, in the case of a relationship, an identification suffix has to be added if another person attributes affect to a relationship in which he is not involved himself. For instance:

My mother thought/	M_i
that I liked my fiancé./	$(I - F+)_{M_i}$

The suffix M_i is added to make clear that this is the mother's (M_i) perception of the situation. The same applies to direct quotations of what other persons said, such as:

Then my mother said to me,/	$M_i - I$
'Don't tell your fiancé/	$(I-F)_{M_i}$
that I told you anything.'/	$(M_i - I)_{M_i}$

However, if the sentence reads:

My mother said to me/	$M_i - I$
that I shouldn't tell my fiancé about this,/	$I - F$

it is coded in the usual way since it is reported in terms of the interviewee's perception of the total situation.

Pronoun Coding

We have already referred to the fact that, where pronouns are used, the person or persons referred to have to be explicitly specified in the code. In a competently carried-out interview, this will not present difficulties for pronouns such as he, she, we, or they.

The pronoun 'you', however, is essentially ambiguous, and its possible reference meanings need to be discussed. The pronoun 'you' may be used in any one of the following ways:

1. I said to my boy friend,/	$I - C_i$
'You may do this/	C_i
if you want to.'/	C_i

'You' in this case refers to the other person.

2. I wasn't much for hitting the books,/	$I -$
and the boys that roomed with me complimented me/	$C_i - I+$
because they were the same way./	C_i
In other words, if you got home at 12.00 to 1.00/	(IC_i)
you'd open up a book/	(IC_i)

and you'd get your studying done during
lunch,/ (IC_i)
and that's what we did./ (IC_i)

'You' refers to the 'we' composed of self and roommates,
and is used in the sense of 'if you were one of us, you would do
this'.

3. If my father feels a certain way,/ P_i
   you can talk yourself blue, and/ (IO)
   you're not going to get anywhere./ (IO)

'You' refers to me or any other person.

4. However, in the following case:
   I was sharing a room with these boys and if/ $I - C_i$
   you got home late . . ./ (IC_i)

'You' refers to my roommates or myself, and group coding
cannot here be applied.

5. There is a period when you can't get
   married./ E

'You' refers to everybody in the sense of 'nobody can get
married'.

6. You don't have this custom in New
   England./   (not coded)

'You' is used impersonally, in the sense that this custom does not
exist in New England, and is, therefore, not coded.

The pronoun 'they' is similarly ambiguous and its reference
has to be made explicit and coded in the same way.

Faulty Verbalization

Slips and inadequate verbalizations which are incomplete and
immediately corrected are disregarded in coding. For instance:

The only discussion we had, . . . which I had
with my fiancée's father . . . $I - P_f$

is coded as self to fiancée's father. However, a consistent tendency to use 'we' corrected to 'I', or vice versa, may suggest unresolved identification problems and could be recorded by a separate coding category, for instance: $(W \rightarrow I)$ if 'we' is corrected to 'I'.

CHAPTER 11

From Dating to Marriage
The Longitudinal Phase-transition Technique

———◆———

SUMMARY

The original form of representation of a life-space in terms of adjoining regions has the topological property of limiting the number of common boundaries of regions. Heider (1946) and Bavelas (1948) showed the advantages gained in the way of representation and formal analysis by using point regions which can be linked to one another, a method which has antecedents in sociometry (Moreno, 1934). This method is particularly suitable for representing networks of relations between a set of elements, but discards quantitative information. The form of representation employed in this chapter, referred to as a topometric diagram, uses the size of regions and the length of directed lines to provide a basis for both quantitative and graph theoretical analysis.

The illustrative case-study, based on a joint interview of an engaged couple, shows that the code developed in Chapter 10 makes it possible to record the changes that occur in the life-space structure of each partner as their relationship develops through successive phases leading to the establishment of a family group.

———◆———

THE LIFE-SPACE coding technique will be applied to the analysis of one interview of an engaged couple obtained shortly before their marriage. This was the first of a series of joint and individual interviews which formed part of a longitudinal research study of couples, directed by Dr Rhona Rapoport at Harvard School of Public Health. The present joint interview of the couple was carried out by a male together with a female interviewer, and covers the sequence of events from the time of the first meeting of the couple, through the periods of dating and of their engagement, to the period during which they make their wedding arrangements.

We shall be concerned with what is essentially a social developmental process which goes through a number of distinguishable phases, leading ultimately to the formation of a group.

During each phase a pattern of interpersonal relationships is established while others are relinquished. This provides the essential basis for moving on to the next transitional phase during which more central relationships are relinquished and new ones developed, until, step by step, each one of which implies a deeper personal and mutual commitment, there are established all the necessary structural conditions—both of the interpersonal relationship and of the external social network— that are required for the formation and maintenance of a family group.

It will be shown that the method of analysis makes it possible to determine the boundaries of successive phases in terms of critical transitions within the interpersonal relationship structure, to analyse behaviour and affect trajectories, and, finally, to map out the life-space structure of each member of the couple at each phase of their relationship.

For the purpose of life-space analysis, the interview itself should as far as possible maintain a mid-point between lack of direction (since in this case some regions within the total situation would not be dealt with) and structured interviewing (since this would inhibit and distort the interviewee's spontaneous report of the situation as he experiences it). In practice, it will be preferable to lean towards spontaneity of expression and freely flowing communication but to maintain the direction necessary to cover all relevant aspects of the situation. A general analytical framework to identify the major regions within the total situation will be needed to provide the basic underlying structure of the interview.

These conditions were met rather well by the interview analysed here, although it was not originally designed for the present method of analysis. With few exceptions, the interview, although relatively structured, consists of the spontaneous reporting of events and experiences of the couple. The few instances where specific probing was used, leading to affirmative or negative replies, are excluded from the coding. The couple in this case-study will be referred to as David and Mary.

BEHAVIOUR TRAJECTORIES

Direction of the Bride–Groom Relationship

One of the measures that can be used to determine the extent to which bride and groom have an identical perception of the situation is the extent to which each perceives their interaction relationship as being initiated by the self towards the fiancé(e) $\Sigma(I-F)$ or by the fiancé(e) towards the self $\Sigma(F-I)$.

We define

$$\text{Initiation balance } (I-F\%) = \frac{\Sigma(I-F)}{\Sigma(I-F)+\Sigma(F-I)} \times 100$$

The data obtained are shown in *Table 13*.

The extent to which David sees himself as initiating relationships to Mary $(I-F\%)$ can be compared with the extent to which Mary experiences relationships to be initiated by him $(F-I\%)$. The results obtained are plotted in *Figure 20*.

TABLE 13 PERCEIVED DIRECTION OF THE RELATIONSHIP

	Perceived by David			Perceived by Mary			
	Frequency			*Frequency*			*Discrepancy in perception* %
Phase	*I–F*	*F–I*	*I–F%*	*I–F*	*F–I*	*F–I%*	
Meeting	19	10	66	9	9	50	16
Dating	21	1	95	1	6	86	9
Engagement	5	4	55	19	19	50	5
Wedding arrangements	5	5	50	2	2	50	0

M

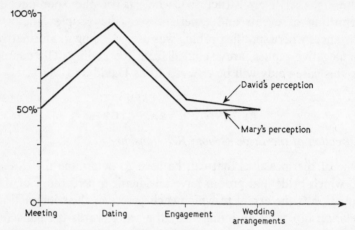

FIGURE 20 BEHAVIOUR TRAJECTORY OF INITIATION BALANCE

There is a slight but consistent tendency for David to perceive himself to be more dominant in initiating relationships than Mary perceives him to be during the initial phases of their relationship. The behaviour trajectories later gradually converge until their perception of the situation in terms of the measure becomes identical shortly before the wedding.

The initiative for arranging the first date had been taken by Mary. This, however, was resented by David. Also, Mary began to feel that the boy should take more initiative, and to consider how she could influence him to act towards her as she wanted him to. Mary puts this as follows:

I always thought, well,/	*I*
I wanted every step that goes with it./	*I*
And so first we went steady/	*W*
and then he gave me a pin and then my hope chest and then my ring./	*F–I*

And somewhat later:

About the pin, he knew,/	*F*
because everybody gets a pin./	*E*

164

But the hope chest, I guess,/	[I]
I must have mentioned,/	$I-F$
and then his boy friend had put in a plug here and there./	C_f-F

At least, during the dating phase, the overt initiative is passed almost entirely to David; however, subsequent to the engagement, an equal balance of initiative is achieved as a steady-state level.

Development of 'We' Feeling

As the relationship of the couple goes through phases of increased emotional and formal commitment, the degree to which a couple identity is established should increase. One measure of this process suggested by Lewin is the degree of 'we' feeling.

Table 14 shows the frequency of references to the self (ΣI), to the fiancé(e) (ΣF), and to we/us (ΣW) referring to the self and fiancé(e).

We define

$$\text{Degree of 'we' feeling } (W\%) = \frac{\Sigma W}{\Sigma I + \Sigma F + \Sigma W} \times 100$$

TABLE 14 DEGREE OF 'WE' FEELING

	David				Mary			
	Frequency				Frequency			
Phase	I	F	W	W%	I	F	W	W%
Meeting	25	11	10	22	16	13	1	3
Dating	16	6	8	25	9	0	4	31
Engagement	12	6	9	34	27	8	13	27
Wedding arrangements	29	9	16	30	8	11	23	35
			Mean W%	28			Mean W%	29

The degree of 'we' feeling is shown in the $W\%$ columns of the table. The increase is far more dramatic in the case of Mary than in the case of David, although the averages for the four phases are almost identical. The results obtained are plotted in *Figure 21*.

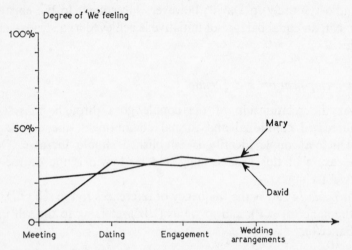

FIGURE 21 DEGREE OF 'WE' FEELING OF THE COUPLE

Mary tends, in this respect, to be more exploratory of the soundness of their relationship, to require both verbal re-assurance and formal evidence from David that he is serious, and to be unwilling to make an emotional commitment until she feels that it will be safe to take each successive transitional step in a firmer mutual commitment.

The day after David had asked her to go steady, which she felt was like being engaged, she reports:

So then the next day, David picked me up,/	$F-I$
and I asked him/	$I-F$
what he felt going steady was,/	F
because I felt it was a big decision/	I
and I wanted to know/	I
how he felt./	F
We discussed it on the way,/	W

and he agreed,/	F
and felt the same way/	F
I did, that going steady was something serious,/	I
didn't you?	[I—F]

At this stage, there is as yet scarcely any 'we' feeling. In Mary's case a real upsurge in 'we' feeling does not occur until they are engaged and they have started on the task of making the wedding arrangements. In her individual interview, she said that all the time she felt that this didn't seem quite real; it didn't seem as if she was getting married. However, during the wedding ceremony, she realized that this was real and that she was now getting married. Whereas, until that time, her emotional tone tended to be flat, after the honeymoon it tended to be lively and elated.

David shows by contrast a completely different pattern. Practically from the start, he accepts a relatively high 'we' identification, which may well be retrospectively inflated[1] and which coexists with and appears to cover up an ambivalent feeling towards his fiancée, compounded of a uniformly negative attitude towards girls in general and an idealized feeling about his fiancée who appears to him so different from all the other girls of his acquaintance.

Reporting on his pre-courtship experience, Davids says:

Before I went to college,/	I
I didn't believe it that much that morals,/	I
and the way that girls were was true,/	G
but especially in my middle years, I had an apartment with three other boys,/	$I-C_i$
and girls, upper classmen, were coming to our apartment three or four times a week/	$G-(IC_i)$
and you didn't have any respect for them—you didn't care that much about them,/	$(IO)-G-$
but it was fun and that was about it./	$I+$

[1] On a number of occasions, David starts off a sentence with 'we', and then, finding that it is inappropriate in the context, switches over to 'I' or 'she'. This code category would appear to provide a measure of the extent to which the 'we' feeling is forced or defensive.

To find a girl (the fiancée) who was in college,/	$I-F$
and even though she wasn't at home,/	F
she would tell you point blank/	$F-I$
'No apartment interests me and I don't care'/	F
I gave a lot of credit and a lot of respect to./	$I-F+$

For David, who has already, from the start, adopted a high 'we' commitment, relatively little further exploration of his partner and their relationship occurs, and there is only a slight increase in 'we' feeling. When Mary reaches her peak of 'we' identification at the time when they are making their wedding arrangements, David begins to show, if anything, a slight decline, showing that they are beginning to be out of step. During the wedding ceremony, he feels that this doesn't seem quite real. Whereas, previously, his feeling tone tended to be relaxed, after the honeymoon, in contrast to Mary, he appeared quite depressed.

TABLE 15A 'WE' IDENTIFICATION BY DAVID

'We' refers to:	'We' identification with:	Phase				
		Pre-courtship	Meeting	Dating	Engagement	Wedding arrangements
(IC_i)	Boy friends	10				
(IG_i)	Girl friends	2				
(IP)	Father	1				
G_f–W	Couple		1			
W			10	8	9	16
W–(M_iP_i)						1
W–P_i						1
(IM_iP_i)	Own family					1
R_i–(IM_iP_i)						1
(IR_i)						1
(IO)	Neighbourhood				1	

TABLE 15b 'WE' IDENTIFICATION BY MARY

'We' refers to:	'We' identification with:	Phase			
		Meeting	Dating	Engagement	Wedding arrangements
(IG_i) } Girl friends		4			
(IG_i)–F		1			
G_i–W } Couple		1			
W		1	4	13	23
(IC_{if})	Boy friends		3		
(WC_f)	Threesome			1	
(IM_iS_i) } Own family				1	
(IM_iP_i)					1
(IM_i)					9
M_i–W } Couple					1
(M_iP_i)–W					1
W–R_f					1

'We' Identification and Transition Phases

So far, we have referred to 'we' identification only in so far as this refers to the couple. In this section, we shall show how changes in the total pattern of 'we' identification for each partner over time can be used to map out the phase structure of his or her developmental process, and to determine the location of his or her transition boundaries.

Tables 15a and *15b* show what the term 'we' refers to in the case of David and Mary. Clear-cut and systematic shifts in the pattern of 'we' identification will be noted over successive phases in their relationship.

In the case of David, the change across phases is quite abrupt. During the pre-courtship phase, 'we' refers primarily to himself and his male friends, with an occasional reference to himself and his girl friends and himself and his father. From the time of his

TABLE 16 STAGES AT WHICH THE CRITICAL TRANSITIONS
WERE MADE IN TERMS OF THE 'WE' IDENTIFICATION

	By David	By Mary
Dissociation from previous partner of opposite sex	Meeting	Engagement
Dissociation from previous partner of same sex	Meeting	Dating
Establishment of predominant couple 'we'	Meeting	Engagement
Establishment of 'we' relationship towards parents	Wedding arrangements	Wedding arrangements

meeting with Mary, his account shows an exclusive use of 'we'
to refer to himself and Mary. The meeting, dating, and engagement phases are, for him, quite undifferentiated, and he
experiences no apparent transition points in terms of shifts in
allegiance during this period. A transition phase occurs when
the wedding arrangements are made, when both their families
begin to be involved in their relationship, and the 'we' referring
to himself and his family becomes activated.

In the case of Mary, we find, on the other hand, a clear
differentiation between each phase, which checks with her
report that, for her, each step in their relationship was a
significant transition point. At the time of their meeting, 'we'
refers predominantly to herself and her girl friends. At the
dating stage, it refers to her and David, and to her and an earlier
boy friend who enters into the relationship at this stage. Once
the engagement phase is entered into, 'we' refers almost entirely
to herself and her fiancé. During the wedding arrangements
phase, we note that, as in the case of David, identifications with
her family are activated, and, for Mary, this applies especially
to her close relationship with her mother.

The data make it possible to go beyond the postulation of
transition phases in the courtship and marriage relationship

to the empirical determination of the phases that exist for each person.

They make it possible further to establish the stages at which critical task transitions are made, based on the analysis by R. N. and R. Rapoport (1965) of essential task requirements which have to be met for the establishment and maintenance of an adequate marriage relationship. The stages at which critical transitions were made by David and Mary are shown in *Table 16*.

All the necessary critical transitions with respect to these four tasks were made by both. Convergence with respect to task achievement occurred by the time of the wedding arrangements phase.

Functions of the Wedding Ceremony: Transitional Re-identification, Separation, and Reconnection

What was rather unexpected in the data discussed so far was the reactivation of family identifications in the phase preceding the wedding. There are both social situational requirements and psychological needs for this. At this stage, the two families relate to one another in the organization of the wedding rituals and in deciding what support each will give the couple. Thus these tasks give the two families and the couple an opportunity to work through their relationships with one another.

At the psychological level, transitional re-identification with one's own family plays an important and essential role in working towards separation. This is best explained by contrasting a wedding, with its social ritual, and an elopement, where families are rejected. Rejection, however, is not separation. Rejection based on dislike or hate maintains or may even increase the attachment. At this stage, working through and separation are not possible until what is rejected is first reaccepted as part of the self and then separated from. It is this reacceptance as part of the self of what one wants to separate from that is referred to here as transitional re-identification.

This may help to explain one of the functions of the wedding ritual. Those who are invited are the family members and friends with whom a prior 'we' identification exists. At the wedding ceremony, it is not only the bride and groom who have to work through and accept the separation, but also the members of the audience. The wedding ceremony in this case provides the condition for transitional re-identification, that is the recognition and acceptance of previous 'we' identifications, and, by attending and playing a supporting part in the wedding, those who are present also demonstrate their acceptance of the separation. Separation, however, does not merely mean a severance of ties but it is itself an essential transitional stage towards reconnection in a new way. After the wedding ritual, the couple can relate as a formally sanctioned 'we' to their family and friends, each of whom is permitted to recognize and accept the new relationship and relate to the couple as a group entity.

AFFECT TRAJECTORIES

Affect trajectories may be determined for any person or group towards whom affect is expressed. In the following, we shall be chiefly concerned with feelings expressed about the fiancé(e) and the relationship to the fiancé(e), and with affect experienced by the subject.

1. Measures of affect experienced by the subject are based on the coding category $I+$ and $I-$.
2. Measures of affect associated with the fiancé(e) and the relationship with the fiancé(e) are based on coding categories

$$F+ve, \; F-ve, \; I-F+, \; I-F-, \; I-F_x+, \; I-F_x-.$$

The affect trajectory with respect to a person is defined as the cumulative affect associated with that person. Each positive affect is given the value $+1$, and each negative affect is given the value -1. If, for a given phase, the sequence of manifest affect obtained from the interview is $-1, \; -1, \; +1, \; +1$, then, with use of zero as a conventional starting-point, the affect trajectory for the phase would be the cumulative values 0, −1, −2, −1, 0.

In order to facilitate the interpretation of the results, the possible types of affect trajectory that may be obtained will first be considered.

Types of Affect Trajectory

A distinction can be made between decontrolled and controlled trajectories. The term decontrolled will be used to refer both to an inability to control and to actual choice not to control. We then have:

1a. Decontrolled positive affect, if all affect is positive.
1b. Decontrolled negative affect, if all affect is negative.
2. Controlled affect, if over a period of time the trajectory oscillates between positive and negative affect.

R. N. Rapoport (1956) and F. E. Emery[1] have suggested that, in primary groups and sustained couple relationships, affect will tend to go through cycles of positive and negative affect. Since the present method makes it possible to obtain affect trajectories for each person, we may go one step further and investigate how the affect states of persons are coupled to one another.

An oscillating controlled trajectory will result if both accumulation of positive affect and accumulation of negative affect lead to increased strain, so that a switch-over from one to the other occurs.

For instance, if the existing situation is peaceful, calm, and positive, one member of the group may start to feel uncomfortable and look for something to disagree about, or he may start a fight or stage an incident. From an experiential point of view, the discomfort is due to fear of loss of the self, which leads to compulsive behaviour to create a condition of conflict so that the ego-centred self can be saved, demarcated, and re-established. After a period of griping or fighting, which will

1 Personal communication.

also increase strain, the group will look for something positive and enjoyable which will again allow strain to decrease.

In the theory of simple behaviour systems (Herbst, 1962) the optimal stress parameter defines the amount of experienced opposition between self and environment where strain is absent. Decreases of stress below the optimal level, or increases above it, lead to increased strain. Attempts to control the stress level can, in this case, lead to an oscillating affect trajectory, decreases in stress being countered by increasing it, and increases in stress being countered by decreasing it. The dynamics of a situation where two persons interact, each with his own optimal stress level, have not so far been investigated. Thus far we have described three basic types of trajectory. Of these, only the positive decontrolled and the controlled oscillatory are consistent with group formation and maintenance.

In theory, any one trajectory can change over to another trajectory, in which case the affect system will be referred to as being meta-stable. An example is shown in *Figure 22(a)*, where unqualified positive affect is replaced by unqualified negative affect. This is the type of pattern that would result if a period of infatuation was followed by disillusionment and hate. The opposite pattern is rather less frequent; however, St Paul's conversion from hostility to faith and devotion would be one example. *Figure 22(b)* shows the type of trajectory that would result if a period of doubt towards a person was followed by love and devotion.

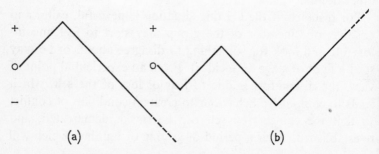

FIGURE 22 ILLUSTRATIVE AFFECT TRAJECTORIES

Each of the basic trajectories can be derived from a linear difference equation model. Changes from one trajectory to another would correspond to changes in the rate of growth parameter in the equation. Coupling of the affect trajectories of two persons could be represented by a set of linear difference equations, where the trajectory of one person was made to lag behind that of the other. For larger groups, it might be preferable to use a simulation model. The model has some analogy to a set of pendulums which are coupled to one another. The methodological problem in this case is how the observed trajectories can be analysed so as to infer how and to what degree the affect states of persons are linked to and influence one another.

Figure 23 shows the personal feeling states of David and Mary, and the feeling of each towards the other. During the initial stages of their meeting, each has a negative defensive attitude towards the other. However, after their first dating experience, a swing to positive feeling by David towards Mary is followed by a swing to positive feeling by Mary towards David by the end of this phase, after which both show a continued accumulation of positive affect until David starts a negative trend during the period when the wedding arrangements are being made.

David's trajectory of his personal feelings is almost the opposite of that of his feelings towards Mary, and shows a continual negative trend after the initial meeting until the final stage, during the making of the wedding arrangements, when a positive upsurging occurs.

Mary's trajectory of her personal feelings is similar, and shows an almost continual accumulation of negative affect. A temporary upward trend by Mary at the end of the dating period has no apparent affect on David. A positive upward surging in the personal feeling state occurs towards the end of the wedding arrangements phase.

In order to obtain a measure of the similarity between the trajectories, the direction of the trajectory will be defined as follows: The direction of the trajectory is said to be positive if

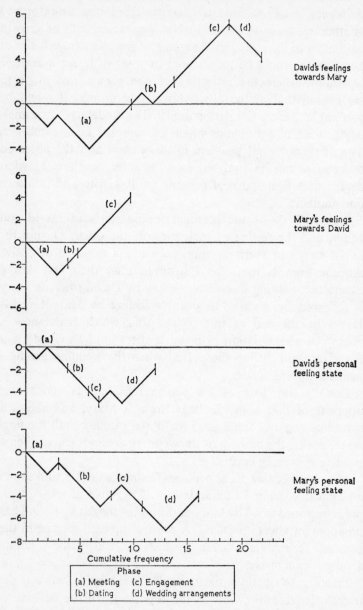

FIGURE 23 AFFECT TRAJECTORIES FOR DAVID AND MARY

its value at the end of the phase is higher than its value at the beginning of the phase; its direction is said to be negative if its value at the end of the phase is lower than its value at the beginning of the phase; it is said to be neutral if the two values are the same. The results obtained are shown in *Table 17*.

The feelings of the couple towards each other are similar during the meeting phase, and identical for the two subsequent phases. The personal feelings of each are identical across all four phases.

What is most interesting and unexpected in this case is that, after the first phase, *whenever there is positive feeling towards the other, there is a negative feeling state of the self, and whenever there is negative feeling towards the other, there is a positive feeling state of the self.* This is true of both David and Mary.[1]

I would hazard a guess that this phenomenon may be found to be an inherent aspect of romantic love, which, as a model, can be traced back to the teaching of the medieval church that

TABLE 17 DIRECTION OF THE AFFECT TRAJECTORIES

	Phase			
	Meeting	Dating	Engagement	Wedding arrangements
David's feelings about Mary	0	+	+	−
Mary's feelings about David	−	+	+	No data
David's personal feelings	−	−	−	+
Mary's personal feelings	−	−	−	+

[1] Rosenman (1955) has noted the reverse phenomenon. As a result of therapy, positive self-evaluation tended to increase while the positive evaluation of others decreased. It would appear to be worth while to follow up this lead by a longitudinal study of individual cases under therapy.

the development of love towards others should go along with and be supported by the recognition of oneself as a miserable, worthless person. In other words, all good aspects of oneself are projected, leaving only the negative aspects for oneself. This may possibly be justified as a transitional stage under certain conditions, but it appears to have become the basic model for the secularized personal romantic relationship.

If we go back somewhat further, we find that the conception of love expressed in both the Old and the New Testaments is of a fundamentally different form, being based on the principle of loving others as one loves oneself. The love of self is here made a necessary and supporting condition for the love of others, and the stage to be achieved is that of equalizing the two, which implies that the distinction between self and others partially disappears at this point. In the more practically oriented Buddhist teaching, the term *metta*, corresponding approximately to 'loving-kindness', is used. *Metta*, it is taught, has to be developed first towards the self before it can be extended towards all beings, and has to be brought to a state of equality in respect of the self and others. Love in the sense of *metta* cannot, however, coexist at the same time with sexualized romantic love. In other words, the existence of the one excludes the existence of the other. This means that they have to be looked at as two dynamically different types of system structure which are antagonistic in the sense that they cannot coexist at the same time.

We cannot exclude the possibility of other different types of love. However, we can make a distinction at this stage between the following:

1. Love in the sense of *metta*, where love towards the self is the basic supporting condition for love towards others, and which reaches its aim when the two are equalized.
2. Personal romantic love, which may be sexualized to a greater or lesser extent, and where negative feelings towards the self provide the basis for the development and maintenance of positive feelings towards another person.

The study of affect trajectories in different cultures could provide an empirical basis for determining the possible range and nature of dynamically different types of affect relationship structure.

Affect Balance

So far, we have looked at the individual affect trajectories separately and have found that both the personal and the interpersonal affect states of the couple run parallel. There are some indications that David is the affect leader and that Mary responds by conforming to his affective state; however, the evidence on this point is insufficient and we need an additional analytical technique in order to determine the affect relationship between the couple.

If one partner of the couple expresses positive affect towards the other, this can be reciprocated by positive affect; we may speak in this case of positive mutuality. The expression of positive affect towards the other can be responded to by negative or hostile affect, which we shall refer to as positive contravalence; or the expression of positive affect can be disregarded and not responded to, in which case we shall speak of a positive unbalanced state. The possible outcome states are shown in *Table 18*.

TABLE 18 THEORETICALLY POSSIBLE AFFECT
INITIATION AND RESPONSE PATTERNS

Affect		
Initiated	Responded	Type
+	+	Positive mutuality
−	−	Negative mutuality
+	−	Positive contravalence
−	+	Negative contravalence
+	0	Positive imbalance
−	0	Negative imbalance

N

Since we have to take further into account who initiates and who responds, there are twelve theoretically possible affect response patterns. In practice, it is likely that each couple will manifest only a limited number of these patterns.[1]

The analysis is based on coding categories

$$I-F+, \ I-F-, \ I-F_x+, \ I-F_x-.$$

Affect response is scored if it occurs in the immediately following uninterrupted communication sequence.

The data for the couple are shown in *Table 19*. It will be seen that all of David's expressions of positive affect are reciprocated by Mary. One of his expressions of negative affect is disregarded. However, none of Mary's initiations of positive affect is responded to by David. The dominant affect pattern in this case is one of *positive mutuality initiated by David*. David takes over affect leadership from the start and maintains it for the time being by disregarding affective initiation attempts by Mary. At the same time, the instrumental leadership and effective decision power are gradually taken over by Mary. She is quite frankly concerned with developing and testing techniques for making him do what she wants, and for initiating the type of behaviour towards her that she desires, and although she is worried occasionally that she is not giving David enough authority, she finds that this is not resented by David who is chiefly concerned with pleasing her. Potential conflicts emerge in the area of the social relationships of the couple with their families and friends, which is closely related to the affect relationship area which David seeks to control. However, here also, Mary overrides David's preferences by her final and *de facto* decisions.

Mary, in this case, begins to appropriate both the instrumental and the social-emotional leadership.

Predictions about the future relationship, however, are by no means easy. Its course will depend primarily on the male's

---

[1] Bandura, Lipsher, and Miller (1960) report a study of the three-stage sequence of response to the patient's expression of hostility by the therapist, coded as approach or avoidance, and the subsequent response by the patient, coded in terms of expression of or lack of hostility.

TABLE 19 FREQUENCY OF AFFECTIVE RESPONSE PATTERNS

| Initiation sequence | Initiated affect | Responded affect | Phase | | | Total | Response Pattern |
			Meeting	Dating	Engagement	Wedding arrangements		
David to Mary	−	−	1				1	Negative mutuality
David to Mary	+	+	1	2	1		4	Positive mutuality
David to Mary	−	0				1	1	Negative imbalance
Mary to David	+	0			2		2	Positive imbalance

ability to shape his role. The present case follows, on the whole, the conventional courtship pattern. The man is expected to express his affection to the girl, to which she may respond. At the same time, the man is expected to please the girl and fulfil her wishes. From here on, there are two possibilities. The man may realize that after the honeymoon, when they establish their working relationship as a family, a restructuring of roles has to take place. However, if the male is unable or unwilling to work through this task, at least by the time of the early marriage phase, then no transition will occur, and the pattern established during the courtship phase will become established and perpetuated, leading to a wife-dominant type of family structure.

LIFE-SPACE STRUCTURE

So far, the analysis has been restricted to specific indices of life-space structure and affect. What we are looking for next is some way to represent the total situational structure.

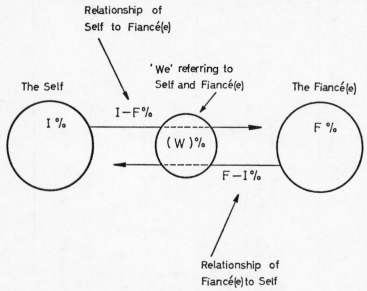

FIGURE 24 LIFE-SPACE STRUCTURE FOR THE SITUATION CONSISTING OF SELF AND FIANCÉ(E)

TABLE 20 FREQUENCY OF CODING CATEGORIES FOR MARY'S
ACCOUNT OF THE MEETING PHASE

Category	Frequency	%	Category	Frequency	%
(I)	5		$I-G_i$	2	3
I	16	25	G_i-I	5	8
$I-F$	9	14	(IG_i)	3	5
$F-I$	9	14	$F-G_i$	2	3
F	13	20	$(IG_i)-F$	1	2
W	1	2	G_i-W	1	2
$I-C_i$	1	2			

The type of diagrammatic representation that will be used is
shown in *Figure 24*. The radii of the circles for the self (I) and the
fiancé(e) (F) give the percentages of references to the self
and the fiancé(e). The 'we' category, referring to self and
fiancé(e) (W), is placed between the self and fiancé(e) regions.
The length of the arrowed rule from self to fiancé(e) represents
the percentage of references to the relationship of self to
fiancé(e) $(I-F)$ and, similarly, the length of the arrow from the
fiancé(e) to the self gives the percentage of references to the
relationship of fiancé(e) to self $(F-I)$.

The resulting diagram can then be extended to include the
remaining coding categories. Since the diagrammatic representation can be analysed as a topological graph but also includes
all the relevant quantitative information, it may be referred to
as a topometric diagram. *Table 20* shows the frequency for each
coding category for Mary's account of the meeting phase. These
are then converted into percentages, disregarding meta-communication categories.

The life-space structures for both David and Mary for each
phase are shown in *Figure 25*. The convention adopted is to
place friends and peers above the self and the fiancé(e) respectively, and family members below them.

DAVID   MARY

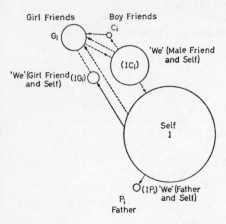

(in the interviews Mary
made no reference to her
life before she met David)

(a) Pre-courtship Phase

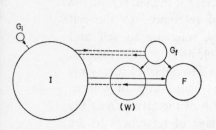

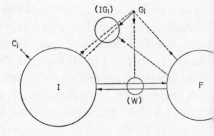

(b) Meeting Phase

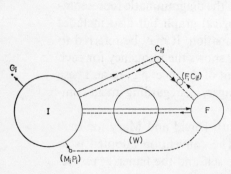

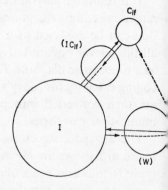

(c) Dating Phase

DAVID   MARY

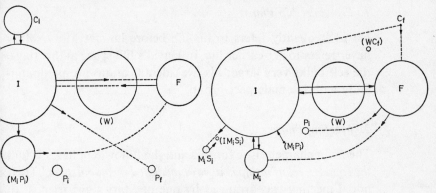

(d) Engagement Phase

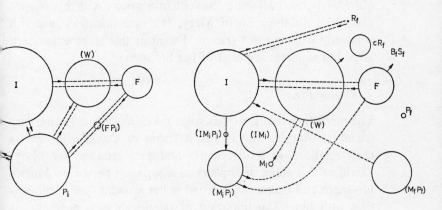

(e) Wedding Arrangements Phase

FIGURE 25 LIFE-SPACE STRUCTURES FOR DAVID AND MARY

1. Pre-courtship Phase

David frequently refers to his life before he met Mary. Mary never refers to her earlier life. In David's life-space at this stage, the self bulks very large; his 'we' identifications are predominantly with his male peer group.

2. Meeting Phase

The main characteristic for this and the following phases is that *the couple's relationship is always mediated by an outsider.*[1] Their initial meeting was arranged by one of Mary's girl friends. In David's life-space, 'we' identification with Mary is developed quite early, and all other 'we' identifications with his friends disappear. In the case of Mary, 'we' identifications are still primarily with her girl friends. David at this stage exists as a large but separate segment of her life-space.

3. Dating Phase

The mediating role is at this stage taken over by a former boy friend of Mary's, who is also a friend of David's. He enters their relationship inadvertently and gets repulsed by Mary. David at this stage disappears as a separate person in Mary's life-space and becomes absorbed in her growing 'we' identification with him. The initiation of relationships is now almost exclusively from David to Mary.

4. Engagement Phase

The relationship of the couple begins to be mediated at this stage by the parents in a positive way. A high level of mutuality has been established by the couple. The initiation of relationships to one another is equally balanced. The relative sizes of the self, other, and 'we' regions in their life-spaces have become

[1] It appears to be true as a general principle that a two-person relationship never exists in isolation. It is either mediated by, or structured with reference to, a third person.

very similiar, and the independent analysis of affect reciprocation shows that a dominant pattern of positive mutuality initiated by David has been established.

5. Wedding Arrangements Phase

The relationship between the couple is now mediated by the parents in a negative way. Mary has a fight and disengages herself from David's father. David is concerned that Mary may be too closely tied to her mother. During this period, when the relationship between their families is worked out, there is a temporary reactivation of the 'we' identification of both with their own family.

At the same time, a critical transition in life-space structure takes place. Their person-to-person relationship almost completely disappears and is now absorbed by their 'we' identification, and it is as an emergent 'we' that they begin to relate themselves to their surrounding world.

CHAPTER 12

Towards a Theory of Cognitive Balance

———◆———

SUMMARY

In the field of social psychology, Heider's principle of cognitive balance (1946) occupies a special position in combining simplicity of formulation with a capacity to explain a wide range of phenomena. A critical analysis of empirical studies by Jordan (1965) shows that it is necessary to demarcate more clearly the conditions under which the principle applies and to seek for an extension of the principle to conditions where at present it does not apply.

As a first step, a distinction has to be made between different types of balance conditions which are related to different prediction problems. Next, a distinction needs to be made between different types of cognitive organization definable in terms of affect (L) and unit (U) relationships.

An approach based on behaviour system theory shows that the like-dislike for different types of evaluative configuration is a function of

   (i) the characteristics of elements
  (ii) the characteristics of the configuration structure
 (iii) interaction effects between structure and elements.

Analysis of available population-study data indicates the type of technique required for testing the theoretical model at the level of individual cases.

———◆———

1. THE CONCEPT of balance when applied to cognitive organizations may refer to any one of the following:

   (a) *Equilibrium balance*: The extent to which a system is in a state of stable equilibrium.
   (b) *Relationship balance*: The extent to which the relationships between the elements of a system are consistent and mutually supporting.

(c) *Affect balance*: The extent to which the system is associated with the type of balance experienced as pleasant feeling and with strain experienced as unpleasant feeling. Affect balance and strain are independent variables (Herbst, 1953, 1962).

While all three are to some extent related to one another, they are not identical.

Heider's principle is defined in terms of relationship balance. If a person p perceives another person o as an enemy, and o disapproves of something p approves of, then the configuration is balanced. Disagreeing about something is consistent with the relationship of being an enemy. However, there is no necessary implication that this is a pleasant state. The evidence reviewed by Jordan shows, in fact, that it is generally rated as one of the least pleasant states. At the same time, the internal consistency of the configuration will contribute to its stability and to its tendency to maintain itself in existence.

2. A distinction has to be made between two types of relationship, which will be referred to as evaluative and attitudinal.

An *evaluative* relationship is one where a given L relationship implies the corresponding U relationship. For instance, if I believe in democracy this means both that I have the belief $(U+)$ and that I feel positively about it $(L+)$. If I don't believe in it, then I do not have the belief $(U-)$ and I feel negatively about it $(L-)$. Finally, if I have no feeling either way about it (L_0), this implies that the belief does not exist as a dynamic element in my life-space (U_0). In a graph representation, this corresponds to the situation where, if a given element does not exist as part of the life-space, a link with the element cannot be established.

The major characteristic of an evaluative configuration is that for a set of elements no more than *one* relationship needs to be specified. The evaluative relationship is dynamically different from the affect relationship. It has the character of 'should' or 'ought'.

3. An *attitudinal* relationship can now be defined as one where the U and L relationships vary independently. This can be the

case for relationships to both objects and activities. Desiring something does not imply that one has it, nor does not wanting to have something imply that one does not have it. Four patterns are possible:

$U+L+$ having something one wants to have
$U-L-$ not having something one does not want to have
$U-L+$ not having something one wants to have
$U+L-$ having something one does not want to have.

The first two patterns are balanced in terms of Heider's definition whereas the two last are not. We shall refer in this case to *object relation balance*.

A relationship to a person may be either evaluative or attitudinal. It is evaluative if the relevant aspect of the relationship is whether he is a friend or an enemy. It is attitudinal if the person exists in the life-space as an object that one wants to have and be together with or not to have and not be together with. The L relationship has the characteristic of desiring an object, an activity, or a state of affairs. Every form of psychological pain and unhappiness is reducible to the condition of wanting something that one does not have or not wanting something that one has.

4. The major characteristic of an attitudinal configuration is that *more than one* relationship between elements is required to specify any given pattern. If only the attitudinal statement 'p likes to own x' is given, this is insufficient to determine the balance characteristic of possible configurations, since this will depend on whether p owns or does not own x.

If the person-person relationship is an evaluative one, but the person-object relationships are attitudinal, then pUx and pLx together with oUx and oLx have to be specified in order to construct a minimally meaningful pattern. The configuration that can be generated in this case is of the following type:

o is perceived as an enemy, and
o has something that p does not have and that both o and p want to have.

This is clearly different from the type of situation where, again:

o is perceived as an enemy, and
o has something that p does not have, o wants to have it, but p does not.

The first is evidently unbalanced in Heider's sense, the latter is balanced.

If only the pUx or the pLx relationship is given, the configuration becomes simply indeterminate. For, if only the pUx term is given, the configurational properties depend on which pLx term is chosen, and, if only the pLx term is given, the configurational properties depend on which pUx term is chosen. If persons are asked to respond to configurations that are indeterminate, and are not given the choice to refuse to respond, they are put in the position of having to add contextual information to make the configuration meaningful. The responses obtained cannot, however, in this case be meaningfully analysed.

In order to study attitudinal configurations, Heider's principle will have to be extended to analyse multi-relationship structures which are at least minimally determinate and meaningful.

5. A distinction has to be made between at least three types of relationship balance:

(a) *Configurational balance*, as defined by Heider's principle.
(b) *Object relationship balance*, defined in terms of discrepancies between liking and having an object, which is a special case of Heider's principle.
(c) *Evaluative or attitudinal balance*, defined in terms of discrepancies in the evaluations or attitudes of p and o.

Both (a) and (c) will be required for the analysis of evaluative configurations. At least three balance criteria will be required for the analysis of attitudinal configurations.

6. There are, then, at least three different type of model which need to be considered in relation to the following problems:

(a) prediction of affect associated with evaluative configurations

(b) prediction of stability of evaluative configurations

(c) prediction of affect associated with attitudinal configurations.

Data are available for the first problem, which will be considered in more detail. Before doing so we need to give more formal and operational definitions of U and L relationships.

DEFINITIONS OF U AND L RELATIONSHIPS

(i) A U relationship is said to exist whenever a set of elements is perceived as forming part of the same unit.

With respect to persons, a U relationship exists whenever p perceives himself and others in terms of 'we' or 'they'.

With respect to person-object relationships, a U relationship exists whenever the object is perceived in terms of 'mine', 'his', 'hers', or 'theirs'.

(ii) An L relationship has the nature of a valence, that is, it has the characteristic of attracting or repulsing and corresponds to the experience of desiring, craving, or greed, and of not desiring, disgust, or hate.

Merely liking something is not sufficient to produce a condition of imbalance or strain. For instance, p might like to be king of England or go to the moon, but not being able to achieve these does not necessarily create a condition of imbalance. A necessary condition for liking to be converted into wanting is that the achievement of what is liked is not perceived as being impossible to obtain.

An attitudinal statement of the type p likes x is indeterminate unless a specific relationship between p and x is stated. If the statement does appear meaningful, this means that contextual information to make the relationship meaningful has been supplied, without its necessarily being realized that this has happened.

For instance, the statement 'John likes cars' communicates a definite meaning. However, this is the case only because the relationship of John to the car which will make the relationship determinate is implicitly supplied, such as 'John likes driving a car' or 'owning a car', and other relationships, such as 'John likes being run over by a car', are implicitly excluded.[1]

(iii) *For every attitudinal configuration, the L relationship has to be defined in terms of the corresponding U relationship.* For instance, if the U relationship refers to having or not having an object, the corresponding L relationship is wanting to keep possession of or not wanting to have the object. If the U relationship is specified as doing or not doing an activity, the corresponding L relationship is wanting or not wanting to carry out the activity because of enjoyment or non-enjoyment of the task.

Unless this rule is adhered to, for any interpretation that appears to be consistent with the balance model any number of other interpretations can be made that will not be consistent with the model.

Throughout the following, p is taken to evaluate himself positively, and p's evaluation of o is taken to be perceived by p as being reciprocated.

EVALUATIVE CONFIGURATIONS

It has been shown so far that there is at least one type of configuration that can be fully specified by a statement of not more than one relationship between any two elements. This

---

[1] The available evidence shows that even with indeterminate statements and configurations highly systematic results are obtained. This suggests that the additional information supplied by different subjects must be very similar. For instance, if the pattern given is

p dislikes o, p likes x, and o dislikes x

the reader may immediately have jumped to the conclusion that the pattern is balanced. If he has done so, this is because he has added the statements 'p has x, and o does not', or he has substituted an evaluative interpretation. If we add 'o has x, but p does not', then the situation is unbalanced.

It would seem worth while to study the way in which incomplete patterns are completed after the response is given. The results should be accountable for in terms of balance theory and will be essential for any theory of linguistic communication.

It may be true that laboratory experiments provide the opportunity to study simplified situations. It does not follow, however, that the results obtained are simpler to interpret.

occurs when the object has the characteristics of a value (*v*) and when the interpersonal relationships can also be taken as being purely evaluative—that is, the question of changing the social relationship to the other person does not arise. We shall assume further, for the time being, that there are no formal, legal, or task-conditioned ties between *p* and *o*, a condition that will be approximately satisfied by informal relationships between peers in non-work settings.

There is at least one study of this simplest of *POV* triads by Hershkovitz (1954), which has been further analysed in detail by Jordan (1965). Subjects were in this case asked to consider all combinations of relationships of self and another person with regard to a value about which each may feel very positive (+2), moderately positive (+1), neutral (0), moderately negative (−1), strongly negative (−2). The other person could be a friend (+2), an enemy (−2), or neutral (0). Data were obtained for sixty situational patterns from twenty subjects who rated each pattern in terms of affect on a 100 mm. scale. These values have been converted to a scale which runs from −100 (most disliked) to +100 (most liked).

Prediction of the Direction of Affect

Table 21a shows the mean affect values for strong evaluations. The three-negative pattern is excluded. Following Heider (1946), this pattern would be expected to be intrinsically unstable so that it would not normally be found to maintain itself in existence in real-life situations. This view is supported by the fact that this pattern stands out as one for which a comparison of different studies shows that stable ratings are not as a rule obtained.

Testing out first of all Heider's configuration measure given by the product of +, − signs, it is found that all unbalanced patterns are rated on the average as unpleasant; balanced patterns, on the other hand, are not necessarily pleasant.

Let us consider next the effect of whether *p* and *o* are in agreement in their evaluations of *v*, which will be referred to as *evalua-*

tion balance. Here again we find that all unbalanced patterns are
on the average rated as unpleasant, but patterns which are in
balance in terms of evaluation are not necessarily pleasant.

Identical results were obtained for the corresponding weak
evaluation patterns shown in *Table 21b.*

Clearly, neither of the criteria provides an effective prediction
of affect. Let us see where each of them breaks down.

The configuration balance criterion breaks down because
being in a state of disagreement with an enemy may be balanced

TABLE 21A STRONG EVALUATION PATTERNS

Mean affect	Pattern p_o p_v o_v	Configuration balance	Evaluation balance	Degree of balance	Degree of imbalance
+94·8	+2 +2 +2	Yes	Yes	2	0
+74·4	+2 −2 −2	Yes	Yes	2	0
−24·4	−2 +2 +2	No	Yes	1	1
−36·4	−2 +2 −2	Yes	No	1	1
−56·4	−2 −2 +2	Yes	No	1	1
−60·4	+2 −2 +2	No	No	0	2
−63·6	+2 +2 −2	No	No	0	2

TABLE 21B WEAK EVALUATION PATTERNS

Mean affect	Pattern p_o p_v o_v	Configuration balance	Evaluation balance	Degree of balance	Degree of imbalance
+79·6	+2 −1 −1	Yes	Yes	2	0
+77·2	+2 +1 +1	Yes	Yes	2	0
−15·6	+2 −1 +1	No	No	0	2
−16·6	−2 −1 +1	Yes	No	1	1
−17·2	−2 +1 −1	Yes	No	1	1
−17·6	−2 +1 +1	No	Yes	1	1
−27·4	+2 +1 −1	No	No	0	2

p_o = p's evaluation of o; p_v = p's evaluation of v; o_v = o's evaluation of v. The
degree of balance is given by the number of criteria that are in balance.

O

but it is not a pleasant state. We note also that being in agreement with an enemy while unbalanced is actually a less unpleasant state.

The evaluation balance criterion breaks down because agreement is pleasant, in fact highly pleasant, with a friend; it is unpleasant, however, to be in positive agreement with an enemy.

If we put both of these criteria together, we find:

Principle 1a: If the triad is balanced both with respect to its configuration and with respect to evaluations of v, then it is experienced as pleasant. If either the configuration or the evaluations are unbalanced, then it is experienced as unpleasant.

Now a perfect prediction is obtained with respect to the direction of affect for both strong and weak evaluations.

We can, in fact, go on a step further. If we measure the degree of balance in terms of the number of criteria that are in balance, which may be zero, one, or both, then a perfect prediction is obtained of the associated affect in terms of three corresponding degrees of affect in the case of strong evaluation patterns. The results for weak evaluation patterns show one deviant case: four of the rated values of unpleasantness are in this case too close together to provide sufficient discrimination.

Prediction of the Rank Order of Affect

The analysis so far would seem to suggest that if the configuration and evaluation balances were combined the degree of affect of possible *POV* triads could be predicted. This turns out not to be the case. Surprisingly, and this is by no means evident from the data considered so far, an analysis of variance of the total data carried out by Jordan shows that a significant independent source of the pleasantness or unpleasantness of the configuration is simply whether o is a friend or an enemy. Further, whether v is positively or negatively evaluated has some effect as well. There are thus four different characteristics of *POV* triads which can be used to predict the degree of affect, which are:

1. configuration balance
2. evaluation balance
3. the valence of *o*
4. the valence of *v* for *p*.

There is little point in selecting one characteristic of a configuration as the best theory. Since all four criteria are logically independent, the problem we are faced with is that of constructing a model which integrates all of them. This can be done within the framework of behaviour system theory.

Perhaps one of the main contributions of system theory is the integration it provides of two previously opposed points of view. The early elementarist approach operated on the assumption that psychological phenomena could be explained in terms of the characteristics of their elements. The subsequent opposite viewpoint was that psychological phenomena had to be explained in terms of the configurational structure of elements. Both points of view are true in the sense that, where the interdependence of phenomena is weak, the elementerist model is applicable, whereas, if interdependence is strong, then the configurational properties are dominant and the element properties are weak, as for instance in transposition phenomena. System theory integrates the two viewpoints by stating that behaviour (B) is a function both of the component elements (C) of a given system and of the way in which the elements are linked to one another (G):[1]

$$B = f(C,G)$$

Since the effect of the elements or of the configuration may disappear, and provided all terms of the equation can be expressed in terms of the same variable, then the equation will take the additive form

$$B = k_1C + k_2G + f(k_1k_2CG)$$

[1] It can be shown within behaviour system theory that the principle logically implies Lewin's principle, $B = f(P,E)$, since, given a simple behaviour system and parametric steady-state conditions, any two stated variables are sufficient for behaviour to become determinate.

As k_1 approaches zero, only the configuration will determine behaviour. Similarly, as k_2 approaches zero, only the component characteristics will determine behaviour. We are concerned with the prediction of the affect associated with a given situation as a function of the affect characteristics of the elements and the affect characteristics of the relationship structure. Since all terms of the relationship are expressible in terms of the same variable, the conditions for an additive relationship are satisfied.

We can now state

Principle 1b: *The affect associated with a cognitive organization will be a function of the affect associated with the elements of the organization, of the affect due to the relationship between the elements of the organization, and of possible interaction effects of the elements and the organizational structure.*

The next step is to formulate measures of both the elements and the structural characteristics of *POV* triads, which contribute to the experienced positive and negative affect.

1. *Valence of Elements*

The elements are:

p_o p's evaluative affect with regard to o

p_v p's evaluative affect with regard to a given value or belief

o_v o's evaluative affect with regard to the same value or belief.

With respect to the elements of a configuration, the pleasantness of the situation will depend on whether o is perceived as a friend or an enemy, and also on whether what is evaluated is perceived as positive or negative. o's feelings, while not irrelevant, will, for the purpose of a first approximation, be disregarded at least with respect to their direct effect on p's feeling state.[1]

[1] There are indications that being with a person who feels positively and is happy about things may not contribute very much to one's own feelings of happiness except for a minority who are able to share other people's happiness. Being with a person who feels negatively or is depressed may, however, have a more immediate negative effect on oneself. The analysis of variance results shows no significant effect. Data inspection shows a relatively small but systematic effect.

2. *Evaluation Balance*

In terms of relationships between elements, strain can arise if p and o make different evaluative judgements and are thus in a state of disagreement. Evaluation balance is represented by the product $p_v o_v$, which is positive if p's and o's evaluations are both positive or both negative. The product is negative if their evaluations are in opposite directions.

3. *Configuration Imbalance*

The second type of relationship between elements is that given by Heider's configuration balance and here we shall assume that *configuration balance does not contribute to pleasant feeling but imbalance does contribute to negative feeling*.

There are two imbalance conditions which need to be considered:

1. being in disagreement with a friend
2. being in agreement with an enemy.

With the symbols

$$p_{o+} \text{ positive evaluation of } o$$
$$p_{o-} \text{ negative evaluation of } o$$

then $p_{o+}|o_v - p_v|$ gives the strain due to discrepant evaluations in the case of a friend

and $p_{o-}|o_v + p_v|$ gives the strain due to consonance of evaluations in the case of an enemy.

The data suggest the need for an additional term:

$p_{o+}p_{v+}|o_v - p_v|$ which denotes the strain due to disagreement with a friend about a matter which p evaluates positively (p_{v+}).

Adding all the above terms, we need to introduce parameters and obtain for the affect (L) associated with a cognitive organization

$$L = \alpha p_o + \beta p_v + \delta p_v o_v - \gamma p_{o+}(1 + p_{v+})|o_v - p_v| - \varepsilon p_{o-}|o_v + p_v| \ldots\ldots(1)$$

TABLE 22A   AFFECT RANK ORDER FOR STRONG EVALUATION PATTERNS

Mean affect	Pattern			$3p_o$	p_v	$3/2p_o o_v$	Configuration imbalance	Total	Rank		
	p_o	p_v	o_v						Theory	Actual	Difference
+94·8	+2	+2	+2	+6	+2	+6		+14	1	1	0
+74·4	+2	−2	−2	+6	−2	+6		+10	2	2	0
+32·4	0	+2	+2	0	+2	+6		+8	3	3	0
+23·6	0	−2	−2	0	−2	+6		+4	4	4	0
−6·0	0	+2	−2	0	+2	−6		−4	5	5	0
−24·4	−2	+2	+2	−6	+2	+6	−8	−6	6	6	0
−27·2	0	−2	+2	0	−2	−6		−8	7	7	0
−36·4	−2	+2	−2	−6	+2	−6		−10	8	8	0
−56·4	−2	−2	+2	−6	−2	−6		−14	9	9	0
−60·4	+2	−2	+2	+6	−2	−6	−32	−34	10	10	0
−63·6	+2	+2	−2	+6	+2	−6	−48	−46	11	11	0

TABLE 22B AFFECT RANK ORDER FOR WEAK EVALUATION PATTERNS

Mean affect	Pattern						Configuration imbalance	Total	Rank		
	p_o	p_v	o_v	$3p_o$	p_v	$3/2p_op_v$			Theory	Actual	Difference
+79·6	+2	−1	−1	+6	−1	+1½		+ 6½	2	1	−1
+77·2	+2	+1	+1	+6	+1	+1½		+ 8½	1	2	+1
+33·6	0	+1	+1	0	+1	+1½		+ 2½	3	3	0
+18·8	0	−1	−1	0	−1	+1½		+ ½	4	4	0
− 2·2	0	+1	−1	0	+1	−1½		− ½	5	5	0
−12·4	0	−1	+1	0	−1	−1½		− 2½	6	6	0
−15·6	+2	−1	+1	+6	−1	−1½	− 8	− 4½	7	7	0
−16·6	−2	−1	+1	−6	−1	−1½		− 8½	10	8	−2
−17·2	−2	+1	−1	−6	+1	−1½		− 6½	8	9	+1
−17·6	−2	+1	+1	−6	+1	+1½	− 4	− 7½	9	10	+1
−27·4	+2	+1	−1	+6	+1	−1½	−16	−10½	11	11	0

For the purpose of predicting the rank order of patterns we do not need to estimate all the parameters. At least one parameter can arbitrarily be set at unity. We can in the present case set $\beta = \varepsilon = 1$, and fit the expression by estimating the three parameters α, δ, and γ. For the present data, feelings about a person have a far stronger effect than feelings about a belief $(\alpha > \beta)$, and disagreeing with a friend contributes more to the unpleasantness of the situation than being in agreement with an enemy $(\gamma > \varepsilon)$.

Tables 22a and *22b* show the index values and rank orders obtained for $\alpha = 3$, $\delta = 3/2$, and $\gamma = 2$.

Table 22a gives the results obtained for strong positive and negative evaluations in situations where a friend, a neutral, or an enemy is involved. The theoretical rank order obtained is in complete agreement with the empirical values.

Table 22b gives the corresponding rank order for weak positive and negative evaluations. The range of affect responses for weak evaluations is markedly smaller than that for strong evaluations. When this is taken into account, the fit obtained is almost equally satisfactory. It will be noted that the departure from a perfect fit occurs when a number of patterns were given almost the same mean rating. The index values for these three patterns, while not identical, are quite close together.

In both tables, patterns with a positive theoretical index have in every case a positive affect rating and patterns with a negative index value have in every case a negative affect rating.

There is one remaining condition to which the model in its present form is not applicable, namely where both p and o make a positive or a negative evaluation, but their evaluations differ in intensity. In this case the evaluation balance criterion does not work since the situation cannot be characterized in terms of either agreement or disagreement, and Heider's configuration balance criterion is not applicable.

Table 22c (p. 206) shows the results obtained. It will be seen that the major part of the variance is in this case taken up by whether o is a friend, a neutral, or an enemy. For the purpose of rank-order prediction, the affect due to differences in the intensity of evaluations has to be taken into account and a measure of intensity imbalance is needed. This is likely to be of particular importance for interpersonal evaluations since if, for instance, p is intensely in love with o, but o only moderately likes p, this contributes a good deal of strain to the relationship. Differences in the intensity of negative feelings, on the other hand, are not a condition of imbalance.

INTENSITY IMBALANCE

We are concerned here with conditions where both p and o agree in the sense that both make a positive or a negative evaluation, but the intensity of their evaluations differs.

Positive Evaluations

The possible positive evaluation patterns are shown in *Figure 26*. If p is strongly attached to a value but his friend is only weakly so, then the situation is unbalanced. If o, however, is an enemy, then the situation is balanced.

If p is only moderately in favour of something but his friend is strongly in favour, then the situation from p's point of view is balanced. If o is an enemy, then the situation is unbalanced.

Algebraically, the condition of intensity balance for positive evaluations can in this case be put in the form

$$p_o(o_{v+} - p_{v+})$$

Negative Evaluations

If both p and o make negative evaluations, then the situation will be balanced whether they are friends, neutral, or enemies. However, the degree of balance will differ depending on whose feelings are most intensely negative.

If p is strongly opposed to something and o is weakly so, then the situation is in relatively strong balance. If o is strongly opposed to something to which p is only weakly opposed, then the situation is in relatively weak balance.

For negative evaluations, the condition of intensity balance is given by the expression

$$p_{v-}(o_{v-} + p_{v-})$$

As before, if o is a friend and p is strongly in favour of something, then if o differs in his evaluation, additional strain is caused. This corresponds to the expression

$$p_{o+}p_{v+}(o_{v+} - p_{v+})$$

The rank-order equation for the degree of affect now becomes somewhat simpler. Affect depends only on

(a) the valence of o and v for p, and
(b) the degree of intensity balance or imbalance.

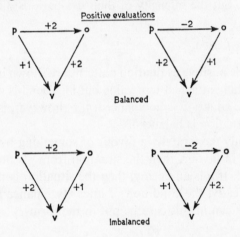

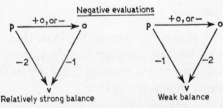

FIGURE 26 BALANCED AND UNBALANCED PATTERNS THAT RESULT WHEN THE 'PERSON' AND 'OTHER' BOTH MAKE A POSITIVE OR A NEGATIVE EVALUATION, BUT THEIR EVALUATIONS DIFFER IN INTENSITY

When all the terms are added, the equation obtained for the affect (L) is very similar to that for equal intensity evaluations:

$$L = \alpha p_o + \beta p_v + \delta'(p_o + p_{o+} p_{v+})(o_{v+} - p_{v+}) + \varepsilon' p_{v-}(o_{v-} + p_{v-}) \quad ......(2)$$

The parametric values for α and β are the same as before. We set $\delta' = 1$.

Table 22c shows the results obtained by estimating $\varepsilon' = 2/3$. The data are accounted for without error. However, two sets of theoretical values in the intermediate affect region are tied.

It should be noted that the equations considered so far are not suitable for quantitative prediction. In order to construct a functional equation all terms have to be made dimensionally homogeneous, which means that we have to find suitable divisors for each balance term. However, it is scarcely worth while to go much further on the basis of population data; it seems better to wait until a few good individual case-records become available.

The present further analysis of the data supports the conclusions arrived at by Jordan. In spite of the abstract and immaginary situations studied in the 'laboratory' setting, together with the summation of results from different individuals, there are strong indications from the data that we are on the track of a general law.

The results could not have emerged from a population study without a quite high homogeneity of parametric values, together with the simple additive structure of the basic components of relationship. Since, however, there are good reasons for assuming that individual parametric differences do exist, the law of affect balance is of Type B form, that is, the functional form of the relationship will be of universal validity while parametric values will vary. It appears possible, though, that parameters can be restricted to positive or zero values.

To go further, it is clearly essential to fit the equation to the data obtained for individual cases. There are in the present case no good reasons why the data from different individuals should be summed together, since each individual case generates

TABLE 22C AFFECT RANK ORDER FOR EVALUATION PATTERNS OF UNEQUAL INTENSITY

Mean affect	Pattern						Total	Rank		
	p_o	p_v	o_v	$3p_o$	p_v	Intensity balance		Theory	Actual	Difference
+52·2	+2	+1	+2	+6	+1	+4	+11	1	1	0
+47·8	+2	-2	-1	+6	-2	+4	+8	2	2	0
+38·8	+2	-1	-2	+6	-1	+2	+7	3	3	0
+28·4	0	+2	+1	0	+2		+2	5	4	-1
+20·4	0	-2	-1	0	-2	+4	+2	5	5	0
+16·0	+2	+2	+1	+6	+2	-6	+2	5	6	+1
+10·8	0	+1	+2	0	+1		+1	7·5	7	-0·5
- 5·6	0	-1	-2	0	-1	+2	+1	7·5	8	+0·5
-10·8	-2	+2	+1	-6	+2	+2	- 2	9	9	0
-14·4	-2	-2	-1	-6	-2	+4	- 4	10	10	0
-16·2	-2	-1	-2	-6	-1	+2	- 5	11	11	0
-17·6	-2	+1	+2	-6	+1	-2	- 7	12	12	0

sufficient data for quantitative analysis. This would make it possible to go on to the study of individual parameters, each of which represents an important personality characteristic. The parameters can be identified as follows:

α   significance attached to interpersonal relationships
β   significance attached to values and ideologies
δ   significance attached to maintaining conformity
γ   tolerance.

We may expect to find that some individuals will find it easier to sacrifice their values to maintain their interpersonal relationships $(\alpha > \beta)$ whereas others will easily sacrifice their interpersonal relationships to maintain their values and ideological commitments $(\beta > \alpha)$.

Parameter γ is the extent to which the imbalance of values and personal relationships arouses strain. For instance, some persons can easily accept a difference of viewpoint without disruption of a friendly relationship, and can tolerate also agreements with an enemy. The *tolerance parameter* γ should be related to the *value commitment parameter* β.

Finally, δ gives the extent to which any agreement *per se* is experienced as pleasant and any disagreement as unpleasant, which suggests that δ can be identified as a *conformity parameter*.

In view of differences in the measurement scales on the basis of which different individuals operate, it will be sounder to base comparative analysis on parametric ratios or inequalities, such as the relative sizes of α and β, than on differences in absolute values obtained.

If possible, moreover, studies should not be restricted to the laboratory setting, which is not well suited for investigating the very real problems of affect dynamics, and for generating the type of data needed for an analysis of individual cases. At the same time, in almost any issues of real concern to human beings, problems of cognitive balance are of relevance and are accessible to study, whether in the field of politics or religion, or in respect of adherence to scientific theories, or with regard to family relationships or the relations between nations, or with regard to the stability of neurotic and psychotic cognitive worlds, as well as in ordinary everyday life. There is thus no reason why each researcher should not choose a problem that is of special interest to him or has particular practical relevance, and in respect of which experimental tests of theoretically possible types of conflict resolution are feasible. Preferably, however, one should at this stage look for situations where patterns take on a relatively simple form.

In this type of work we would start by the systematic study of a total situation existing for an individual, to identify in the first place the actual distribution of evaluative configurations. For each element p_o, p_v, o_v, measures of affect intensities would be obtained, together with the affect associated with the total configuration. The data acquired would make it possible to test both principles of the stability of different configurations and principles of affect balance. The relative frequency and duration of theoretically possible patterns could be used to obtain a measure of the relative stability of each pattern. It would then be possible to test, for instance, the hypothesis that the configuration with three negative signs would not normally appear as a constituent of a life-space.

If such studies are repeated over successive time-periods, additional data for testing theories of change processes would become available. It would be an advantage in this case to choose situations in which the persons and issues involved remained the same over the period studied.

CHAPTER 13

Sense Modalities in terms of Affect Potential and Affect Control

———◆———

SUMMARY

Chapter 11 showed that behavioural universes evolve as a result of successive phases of structure-building. Little, however, is known so far about the conditions that determine the type of behavioural universe that will come into being. One of the conditions that will determine the direction taken by the process of growth is affect arousal and response within the total spectrum of sense modalities.

———◆———

IF WE consider the sense modalities as a potential spectrum of experiences, then individuals may be receptive to only a relatively small range within the total spectrum. Apart from sex differences, which are linked to the dominance of different sense modalities, at least two other factors are likely to be important:

1. Cultural differences provide different dominance hierarchies with respect to each modality, and provide also different encouragements for and sanctions against searching out positive affect in each modality. In some cultures the enjoyment of food is accepted, effort will be channelled into the creation of special dishes, and the taste modality can become both a centre for the development of arts and sciences and an arena for the establishment of status. A person who could not discriminate, appreciate, and be creative in this world of menus and drinks would be judged as incompetent in relevant matters, and in this kind of culture it would seem natural to account for human ills in terms of faulty or harmful nutrition practices,

and most ills would be regarded as curable, at least in theory, by a sustained, proper, and balanced diet, good broth and good red wine. Curiously, this describes an aspect of the English culture of not so very long ago. Today, an inspection of hospital menus shows that medical theory has changed, although there are occasional rumours of medical men in backward rural regions who prescribe stout, red port, and broth for their elderly patients.

2. In the course of development, children explore each of their sense modalities. It seems quite possible that physiological differences provide children with different potentials for deriving pleasure and unpleasure from skin sensitivity, sound patterns, and colour combinations. For some persons colour is just colour. For others, each colour and tone of colour is a rich emotional experience, and some colour combinations and harmonies can create a state of joy and pleasure and others a state of intolerable and painful disharmony. (It need not be repeated that for a person of this type harmonious visual environments will be regarded as having significant curative properties.) What is important, however, is not just the possibility of producing affect in terms of a particular modality but the possibility of controlling affect, and particularly the competence and power achieved in controlling and steering away from conditions of negative affect and in steering towards conditions of positive affect. Thus one child, finding that he can put objects together, acquires a feeling of competence and pleasure, and then expects even greater pleasure by putting more complicated things together; at the same time, he neglects or blocks off other modalities where his attempts repeatedly produce feelings of pain and frustration and which for him do not appear to contain any potential achievable pleasurable state. Since the development of skill and competence is a long process of building progressively more complex structures, and thus creating potentially larger areas and more subtle conditions for pleasure experiences (and, of course, more subtle and complex conditions of frustration as well), then, if

blocking occurs, no further development in this modality is possible at all. A good example is the emotional block that makes it impossible for many persons to use mathematical thinking. The same thing can happen in learning to play musical instruments or in acquiring skill in different sports, except that in our culture the latter is not of the same importance and practical significance.

We may now try to summarize the kind of model implicit in the discussion so far. We may think of each sense modality as varying in terms of the potential amount of pleasurable and unpleasurable feeling that can be derived from it. It is suggested that the difference is not simply quantitative, but that some modalities may be blocked altogether so that defence mechanisms operate to avoid the arousal of feelings since any feeling derived from these modalities is expected to be unpleasant or not capable of being controlled. Thus, blockage of bodily contact may be due to an expected response of unpleasure to any kind of contact or, in the case of adolescents, to the fear of uncontrollable run-away pleasurable feeling that may result.

To the extent that emotional energy is channelled into a sense modality, a process of sequential phases of structural growth will occur. On the one hand, finer discrimination becomes possible and more complex and subtle forms of structure are formed. We would not, then, expect to find a common intelligence factor that carried across different sense modalities, but we would, on the contrary, expect persons to be possibly brilliant in some matters and almost imbeciles with respect to modalities that had become blocked, so that a process of growth and development had never got started. This should apply to almost every other personality characteristic as well. That is, a person may be exact and compulsive in setting out a mathematical proof and terribly upset about any kind of sloppiness, but he may be quite careless and non-compulsive where his or other people's dress is concerned and quite undiscriminating about what kind of food he eats.

P

Given, then, the special capacity that a person has evolved, or his lack of it, this will determine the kinds of social relation into which he can enter, the kinds of condition that will produce stress and discomfort for him, and also the kinds of cure he will look for to reduce unpleasurable feeling.

The type of measurement technique that the discussion suggests is one that will provide quite gross and discontinuous manifest differences with respect to different sense modalities within the same person and between different cultures. We would expect to find quite marked sex differences, and clear qualitative differences for at least certain pathological syndromes. For instance, compulsive-type behaviour should result whenever the possibility of pleasure experience is restricted to some specific condition within one particular sense modality. Thus the so-called sexual pervert, who can get pleasure only from handling a special object under certain specific conditions, will be in a situation where he will be compulsively oriented to try to produce the only condition in which he can obtain a feeling of sensual pleasure, and he will not easily be stopped or diverted by punishment. A mathematician who can derive a feeling of pleasure only from finding a particular form of mathematical structure is dynamically scarcely different from the sexual pervert. The pathological element lies not so much in the intrinsic dynamic structure but in the way in which each of these persons can relate himself socially to others. In a society which did not appreciate mathematical competence, the mathematician might be judged as a kind of madman.

Next, the concept of sense modality has to be extended to include the internal environment, although the distinction is not always easy, since external receptiveness implies accessibility to the internal environment. However, we need to consider that aspect of the internal world that can function independently of external stimuli, and sensual inputs, which include

(a) feelings and emotions
(b) internal fantasies and memories,

each of which constitutes a modality in the above sense, which can be blocked or developed. One interesting difference between Western and Eastern culture is that the former relies for affect control almost entirely on manipulating sensual input from the environment, which means that control of the environment becomes a dominant trend. Eastern culture emphasizes much more direct physiological control of the body in order to manipulate the affects (Yoga), or the temporary blocking-off of the external senses in order to gain direct control of the affects (meditation techniques).

The use of the five basic sense modalities may be inwardly or outwardly directed. In the case of body contact, the same experience may be interpreted as inwardly directed, as being touched, or as outwardly directed, as touching.

	Inward	*Outward*
sight	to see, to watch	to be seen, to be watched, to display
sound	to listen to	to be listened to
touch	to be touched	to touch
smell	to smell	to be smelt
taste	to taste	to be tasted (oral-skin contact)

If we include the internal modalities together with conceptualization, which may operate on the content of any one modality, the matrix can be extended as shown in *Table 23*.

The following are the types of measure that would be relevant and could be obtained by either interview or questionnaire.

1. *Hierarchy of Sense Modalities*

Sense modalities vary in terms of their importance to oneself. The loss of some of them may be regarded as so damaging that life without them will not be regarded as worth while.

The extended set of modalities and related capacities would include:

Taste, sight, sound, smell, body feeling, emotions, intellectual ability, use of arms, use of legs, memory, fantasy and dreams, having the opportunity of being on one's own, having the opportunity of being with others.

TABLE 23 INTERNAL MODALITIES

| | Introverted | | Extraverted | |
	Passive	Active	Inward directed	Outward directed
Emotions	Being receptive to emotional states	Manipulating emotional states	Seeking physical, sensual, or cognitive inputs to modify emotional states	Exploring the inner feelings of other persons; manipulating the affective states of others
Fantasies, memories	Being receptive to fantasies and memories	Directly manipulating fantasies	Seeking physical, sensual, or cognitive inputs to create or modify fantasies	Exploring the inner world of others; guiding and manipulating their fantasies
Conceptual	Being receptive to and understanding of rational logical structures	Formulating theories	Seeking theories, beliefs, and meaningful explanatory systems	Convincing others of one's beliefs and theories; seeking to convert others

2. *Potential for Affect Arousal*

Sense modalities will vary in terms of their capacity for arousing positive and negative affect. Further, the type of affect experienced will to some extent vary for different modalities.

Considering first the negative affects, one would expect disgust and nausea to be related to smell and taste, worry to be related to conceptualization, fear and anxiety to sight and sound.

Positive affect can take two forms. It may be experienced in the form of thrill, excitement, and bodily pleasure, or in the form of calm joy, a feeling of being completely at ease, which may be experienced as an absence of the feeling of bodily weight, and which can be associated with an unbounded love towards all beings, a near-physical perception of light, and a loss of ego feelings, although this last can also appear in conjunction with fear and anxiety.

Each sense modality has to be considered in its active and passive forms. The affect aroused by, say, touching and stroking will be different from that aroused by being touched and stroked. Further, in each case, the external relationship involved may be with an object, with one other person, or with a group, or there may be detachment from external sense objects.

3. *Affect Control*

Affect control will be concerned predominantly with the control of negative affect. However, counteraction to excessive positive affect can also occur owing to fear of attachment to the condition or person that arouses the positive affect and of the potential loss of this condition or person.

The techniques of control of negative affect are practically coextensive with those employed in the field of lay and professional psychotherapy. There appear to be basically three such techniques:

215

1. Arousal of positive affect in the same or another modality to counteract negative affect.
2. Reduction of total affect intensity.
3. Understanding and modification of the internal structural conditions which produce negative affect. Since a good deal of negative affect is secondary and due to fear of content which is blocked and suppressed by the above mechanism, bringing the negative affect fully into consciousness can by itself be effective.

An easily accessible source of data on affect control exists in the field of market research. A technique for studying the use made of various forms of input such as foods, beverages, stimulants, depressants, TV, reading, etc. has been developed by F. E. Emery at the Tavistock Institute of Human Relations.

4. *Control Capacity*

In the course of development, a capacity for building increasingly complex and sophisticated structures will be acquired. What would be of interest at the next stage would be the construction of capacity and control measures for each modality, analogous to intelligence tests. Capacity measures would need to be worked out for each sense modality, and for both passive and active involvement; for instance, appreciation of a musical composition does not imply a capacity for constructing one, although the latter implies the former.

CHAPTER 14

Organizational Commitment
The Longitudinal Dynamic-process Technique

————◆————

SUMMARY

It is frequently said that a qualitative approach to the study of human behaviour is essentially different from a quantitative approach. This may not necessarily be the case. If a systematic qualitative description of a behavioural situation can be achieved, then this description can frequently without any further assumptions be translated into a quantitative form and the logical and quantitative implications obtained can then be used to test the validity and accuracy of the qualitative description. The alternative approach, which has so far been little used, is to start off with quantitative data and use these to infer the qualitative structure of the phenomena studied.

The longitudinal dynamic-process technique discussed in this chapter is not in itself new. The method was originally developed in the field of chemical kinetics and has been applied to diffusion processes both in biological and in social systems. The application of this technique to the study of labour turnover provides an interesting example of a situation, occasionally found in the behavioural sciences, where the conditions for applying a simple physicalist model appear to be satisfied.

I am indebted to Richard Solem, a civil engineer, for the experience I gained in working with him for some time on the construction of interaction models, and to Dr Magnus Hedberg for his kindness in putting photostat copies of his data on labour turnover at my disposal.

————◆————

THERE ARE, generally speaking, two techniques that may be used to study an organization. We may study the organization directly by inspection, and find out what its component parts

This chapter was first published in *Acta Sociologica*, 1963.

are and how these are linked to one another; or we may, without any direct knowledge of the organization itself, acquire data on its input and its output, and use these data to infer qualitative and structural characteristics of the organization.

The first approach assumes that we have access to the organization and are in a position to carry out some form of systematic behaviour-recording, as well as to collect data on the experienced situational characteristics that exist for individual members. These data can, to begin with, provide a qualitative model. At the next stage, the qualitative model may be translated into a quantitative form. Our basic data in this case are qualitative and in the course of data analysis we may arrive at some form of quantitative formulation.

The second approach goes in a sense in the reverse direction. Input-output data in the case of social and industrial organizations are, for instance, the number and type of entrants who come in and leave the organization, the amount and type of material coming in, and the various goods and services produced. Data of this type generally become available in a quantitative form. The transformation of inputs into outputs occurs within the organization itself. The problem then is, can we use the input-output relationships found to infer certain internal characteristics of the organization?

To give an example: In a study of about 400 shops which form part of a retail chain in England, data became available on the output (given by the sales turnover of each shop), the size (given by the number of persons employed), and the input (given by the amount of wages paid).

If a retail shop is relatively small, all employees including the manager will participate in various essential productive activities. Organizations of this type may be referred to as *simple* systems. As the size of the shop increases, the work in the form of task control and social management increases, so that, when a certain critical size is reached, self-regulation breaks down and an administrative unit which will include the manager is separated out. This type of organization may be referred to as a *complex* system. It is found in this case that simple systems differ from complex systems in respect of the form of their input-output functions, therefore the input-output relationships can be used to provide information on certain aspects of the internal structure of the organization and to give some indications as to the types of condition under which intrinsic regulation of social systems breaks down (Herbst, 1957c).

SURVIVAL CURVES

In a series of papers, Rice, Hill, and Trist[1] introduced the first input-output technique for the study of organizations, based on the survival curve of entrants, which is obtained by taking all persons or a specified group of persons who have joined the organization during a given period of time, and recording the number remaining in the organization over successive time-periods. These studies demonstrated the possibility of using data of this type for mapping out the internal boundary structure of an organization, for studying the process of organizational change, and for indicating the capacity of the organization to retain its members. The transformation of the method into a diagnostic technique depends, however, on the possibility of finding a function that will fit the data.

Successive attempts have been made to find a function to fit survival-curve data by Rice, Hill, and Trist (1950), Silcock (1954), Lane and Andrew (1955), and, more recently, by Hedberg (1962). The equations suggested may be put in the general form

$$\frac{dN}{dt} = - N.f(t)$$

The implicit assumptions that were made are:

(i) The rate of decrease in the number of entrants decreases with the number of entrants remaining with the organization (N) and is assumed to decrease also as a function of time.

[1] Rice, Hill, and Trist (1950); Rice (1951); Rice and Trist (1952).

(ii) Every entrant is a potential leaver, in the sense that the only choice he has is to leave.

(iii) The loss of entrants is a single continuous process.[1]

The data collected in British industrial firms had, however, a number of limitations which made it difficult to provide a satisfactory test of the possible functions proposed. The entrant populations studied were often relatively small, the data were generally recorded in three-month periods, and insufficient data were collected to show what happened after the first two years. The available data showed that, at least over the initial two-year period, an empirical function proposed by Bartholomew (1959) provided the best fit. This function has the form:

$$N = N_0 \left[pe^{-\lambda_1 t} + (1-p)e^{-\lambda_2 t} \right]$$

where N is the number of entrants remaining with the organization.

Little further progress could be made until Hedberg, in a remarkable study carried out in Sweden in 1960 (Hedberg, 1962), provided survival-curve data for approximately 40,000 male entrants over sixty successive monthly periods. Data were obtained for entrants over five successive years and categorized for the age of the entrant. In the field of the behavioural sciences, which have up to now had little to show in the way of large-scale systematic and detailed data-gathering, this study may well be considered as an outstanding contribution.

A preliminary analysis of the data showed that, after the first two years, survival curves approach exponentially a constant value, which is therefore easily estimated and is found to vary for the available Swedish data within the range of 14 to 47 per cent of the entrant population.

This means that at least the second hypothesis has to be rejected. In other words, not all entrants are potential leavers. We can conclude that at least some of the original entrants

[1] Retirement on reaching a fixed age-limit is not taken into account in relatively short-run models.

eventually establish some form of permanent and reciprocated commitment to the firm so that they would no longer consider voluntary leaving and would not, in the normal course of events, be considered for dismissal by the firm. These findings suggested that the method might provide a basis for studying the process and conditions leading to what may be called organizational commitment.

Of the proposed functions, the Bartholomew equation again offers a good fit for the data, provided that a parameter is added which gives the number of entrants who ultimately remain with the organization. The function, however, in a number of cases breaks down completely for the first month. This suggested that a more complex function might be needed and indicated that the search for an empirical function might not be worth while. Also, empirical functions, even if these are based on possible statistical models, do not provide parameters that can be meaningfully interpreted. What appeared to be more feasible at this stage was to attempt the construction of a theoretical model based on the actual characteristics of the process by which an entrant establishes a relationship to the organization.

Suggestions for such a model have been made which look at the entrant as going through successive phases in his relationship to the organization.

In the study by Rice, Hill, and Trist (1950), the basic conceptual model employed is that of an open system. The suggestion made is that labour turnover needs to be looked at as a total process extending from sources of entrants to destinations of leavers. The entrant is seen as going through three successive stages: (1) the period of engagement and induction, when he is most likely to go through a crisis and leave; (2) the period of differential transit, when those who remain may become applicants for training or promotion; (3) the period of settled connection, when the entrant establishes his position in the organization and may qualify for long-service benefits.

We may note in this connection that the Bartholomew

function is precisely the type of equation that would result if the relationship of the entrant to the organization went through successive and independent phases.

It did appear remarkable that the type of function proposed by Bartholomew fitted the data over nearly sixty consecutive months but in a number of cases broke down completely during the first month. Could there be something that occurred within a period of approximately one month which might account for the deviation?

One rather obvious and simple solution presented itself, namely, that a new entrant would not normally leave the day after he joined the firm, and also, later on, some period which may exceed one month may elapse between deciding to leave (or being dismissed) and actually leaving. We can now go ahead and construct a qualitative structural model. However, in order to do this we shall, to begin with, need to consider more carefully the successive phases in the development of a relationship between the individual and the organization, which may be looked at in terms of successive stages of increasing commitment to the organization.

A person is frequently said to become a member of an organization subsequent to some form of selection. This type of model is not entirely satisfactory. There are special cases where, following a selection procedure, a mutually binding relationship is established. However, in the majority of cases, the initial formal or informal testing procedure functions as no more than an initial screening and the actual process of selection takes place during the initial period of association, when the entrant will test the organization against his expectations and requirements and be tested in turn by the organization.

Individuals may be looked at as moving from one organization to another until they finally, so to say, get caught and establish a permanent relationship. Some individuals may remain with the first organization they join, others will be transiently attached to several before they settle down, and a remainder may never be able to establish more than a short-term relationship.

Within the organization itself, the entrant group can be looked at as a pool of largely transient associates from whom ultimately a selection of candidates for permanent membership will be made. In traditional institutions this process is quite clearly formalized, for instance in the transition from engagement to marriage or from being a novice monk to taking full orders.

In present-day organizations these formal distinctions are generally less marked with the exception of certain professions and crafts, where, however, the commitment is to the professional or craft organization rather than to the institution where the individual happens to work.

In most cases, formal recognition as a permanent member is frequently no longer binding, and employees may be *de facto* permanent members without a corresponding formal status.

We shall, therefore, in the following consider organizational commitment as a state in which the individual no longer considers leaving the organization and is no longer considered by the organization as somebody who can be dismissed. In an industrial firm, then, a permanently committed member will be anyone who will stay on with the firm until he is pensioned off, dies, or has to retire for reasons of health.

A LINEAR TRANSITION MODEL

The stages leading to commitment may now be set out as shown in *Figure 27*. During the initial period, some or all entrants will be in a pre-decision stage. Either the question of staying permanently has not yet become relevant or the entrant may continue for some time in a state of indecision. During this period, he will explore and become acquainted with his job, his fellow workers, and his superiors, and he will in turn be tested by either informal or formal appraisal for his suitability as an organizational member.

Depending both on his own need to arrive at some decision concerning his future relationship and on organizational pressure, he will sooner or later move into a decision stage.

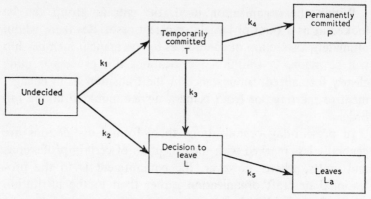

FIGURE 27 THE QUALITATIVE STRUCTURAL MODEL

He may decide that the organization is unsuitable for him or he may be judged unsuitable by the organization. In either case there will be some generally short period which intervenes between the decision to leave and actual leaving.

The alternative decision that may be made is that of establishing a temporary commitment to the organization. The individual will at this stage look at himself as a member of the organization, but will not yet consider himself to be in any sense permanently committed. His position is thus not yet fully established so that at some stage, in which both he and the organization are involved, he has to make the decision either to establish a lasting commitment or to take the remaining course open to him, and back out and leave. It may be noted that leaving at this stage may involve a loss of some form of personal and social investment which he has come to make in the organization.

The model, which is shown in *Figure 27*, can now be translated into a quantitative form. Let:

U = the number undecided or in the pre-decision stage
T = the number temporarily committed
P = the number permanently committed
L = the number who have decided or have been asked to leave

L_a = the number who have actually left
N = the number of entrants remaining in the organization
N_0 = the initial number of entrants
N_p = the number who finally remain as permanent members.

Entrants who are in the pre-decision stage can either go to the stage of temporary commitment or decide to leave. The rate of transition to temporary commitment is $k_1 U$, and the rate of transition to the decision to leave is $k_2 U$. The rate of decrease in the number of entrants who are initially in the pre-decision stage is therefore $k_1 U + k_2 U$. Similarly, the change in the number who are temporarily committed will increase at the rate $k_1 U$ coming from the pre-decision stage, and will decrease with the outflow $k_3 T$ who decide to leave at this stage and $k_4 T$ who go on to the state of permanent commitment.

The coefficients k_1, k_2 ... represent the transition tendency, or what might also be called the transition pressure, which operates in either direction, and this is taken to remain constant over time.

The model thus corresponds to the following set of equations:

$$
\left.
\begin{aligned}
\frac{dU}{dt} &= -(k_1 + k_2)U \\[2mm]
\frac{dT}{dt} &= k_1 U - (k_3 + k_4)T \\[2mm]
\frac{dL}{dt} &= k_2 U + k_3 T - k_5 L \\[2mm]
\frac{dP}{dt} &= k_4 T
\end{aligned}
\right\} \quad \dots\dots(1)
$$

The total number remaining in the organization N will consist of those at the pre-decision stage, those who are temporarily or permanently committed, and those who have decided to leave but have not yet actually left, so that

$$N = U + T + P + L$$

In order to determine the number of persons remaining in the organization at any given time, and the number who will ultimately become permanently committed, the set of differential equations has to be integrated. This presents no difficulties. The solution for a linear transition network will always have the form of a sum of exponentials. The number of exponential terms depends on the number of decision points. In the present model there are three decision points, so that the solution has the form

$$N = Ae^{-\alpha t} + Be^{-\beta t} - Ce^{-\delta t} + N_p \qquad \dots\dots(2a)$$

In the special case where the decision to leave is followed within the period of less than one month by actual leaving, the equation takes the form of the Bartholomew-type function

$$N = Ae^{-\alpha t} + Be^{-\beta t} + N_p \qquad \dots\dots(2b)$$

In order to test the model, the survival-curve data for two of the firms reported in the Hedberg study will be used. Firm A had the highest loss of entrants in the sample of male employees studied, and Firm B the lowest loss. Both firms are iron and steel works. At the beginning of the study, Firm A had 3,846 employees and lost 8,949 over a five-year period; Firm B had 1,544 employees and lost 988 over the same period.

The fitted equation, based on the percentage of entrants remaining with the organization, obtained for Firm A is

$$N = 45 \cdot 44e^{- \cdot 4270t} + 41 \cdot 94e^{- \cdot 0966t} - 2 \cdot 31e^{-10 \cdot 15t} + 14 \cdot 93$$

The last exponential terms δ is calculated from the parametric equations (5) and (8). According to the model, the value of δ should be sufficiently high for the last exponential term to drop out after about a month. This is found to be the case.

For Firm B we obtain

$$N = 12 \cdot 74e^{- \cdot 3608t} + 40 \cdot 25e^{- \cdot 1142t} + 47 \cdot 00$$

Table 24 shows the actual and theoretical values. The fact that a good fit is obtained does not as yet provide sufficient evidence for the model discussed. All it shows is that the decision process can be looked at as going through two or three successive, apparently very nearly independent, stages.

The model requires in addition that the estimated parameters satisfy all of the following parametric equations, which are

TABLE 24 PERCENTAGE OF ENTRANTS 1949–1952 REMAINING
IN THE ORGANIZATION

Month	Firm A 7,628 entrants 1 person = ·01%		Firm B 968 entrants 1 person = ·10%	
	Actual	Theoretical	Actual	Theoretical
0	100·00	100·00	100·0	100·0
1	82·66	82·66	91·7	91·7
2	68·85	68·85	85·1	85·1
3	58·95	58·94	79·8	79·8
4	52·10	51·66	75·6	75·4
5	46·61	46·17	71·7	71·8
6	42·32	41·92	67·7	68·7
7	38·73	38·53	64·9	66·1
8	35·74	35·77	63·0	63·8
9	33·52	33·46	61·3	61·9
10	31·78	31·56	59·5	60·2
11	30·19	29·81	58·5	58·7
12	28·46	28·33	57·2	57·4
13	27·20	27·03	55·9	56·2
14	25·85	25·87	55·4	55·2
15	24·79	24·83	54·8	54·3
18	22·25	22·30	53·1	52·2
21	20·36	20·43	51·4	50·7
24	19·06	19·04	49·7	49·6
27	18·01	18·00	48·8	48·9
30	17·31	17·23	48·2	48·3
36	16·45	16·22	47·7	47·7
42	15·77	15·65	47·4	47·3
48	15·35	15·33	47·2	47·2
54	15·18	15·16	47·1	47·1
60	15·05	15·06		
66	15·00	15·00		

based on the assumption that at the time of entry everyone is at the pre-decision stage ($N_0 = U_0 = 100$):

$$\alpha = k_1 + k_2 \qquad \qquad \text{......(3)}$$

$$\beta = k_3 + k_4 \qquad \qquad \text{......(4)}$$

$$\delta = k_5 \qquad \qquad \text{......(5)}$$

$$A = N_0 \frac{k_5}{\alpha} \left[\frac{k_2(\alpha - \beta) - k_1 k_3}{(k_5 - \alpha)(\alpha - \beta)} \right] \qquad \text{......(6)}$$

$$B = N_0 \frac{k_5}{\beta} \left[\frac{k_1 k_3}{(k_5 - \beta)(\alpha - \beta)} \right] \qquad \text{......(7)}$$

$$C = \frac{N_0}{k_5} (\alpha A + \beta B) \qquad \qquad \text{......(8)}$$

$$N_p = N_0 \frac{k_1 k_4}{\alpha \beta} \qquad \qquad \text{......(9)}$$

In the special case where the interval between the decision to leave and actual leaving is short, for $k_5 \to \infty$, we obtain

$$C = 0 \text{ and both } \frac{k_5}{k_5 - \alpha} \text{ and } \frac{k_5}{k_5 - \beta} = 1$$

The number of entrants who will remain permanently with the organization (N_p) is seen to depend on the tendency to accept a temporary commitment k_1 multiplied by the tendency to accept a permanent commitment k_4 relative to the total decision pressure at each decision point.

The problem now is that, having calculated the transition pressures k_1, k_2, and k_5, we have two sets of equations each of which provides values for k_3 and k_4. Now for the model to hold, these two estimates have to be identical. For Firm A the calculated values for k_3 are ·0685 and ·0659, and for k_4 ·0281 and ·0307. We may take the mean values as the best estimate. In the case of Firm B, the first set of equations gives the value of $k_4 =$ ·0718 and the second set of equations gives again $k_4 =$ ·0718. A similar identical value up to four decimal places is found for k_3. This is an unusually good agreement.

Figure 28 shows the decision-process structure obtained for each firm. In both firms the decision pressure at the first stage is about three to four times as high as the decision pressure at the second stage. However, in Firm B there is a much higher relative tendency to make a permanent commitment. In Firm A there is a relatively higher decision pressure at the start and a greater relative tendency to leave, not only at the first

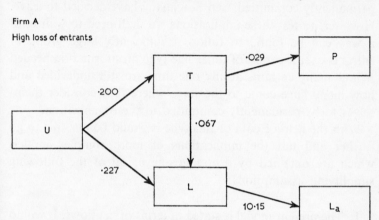

Firm A

High loss of entrants

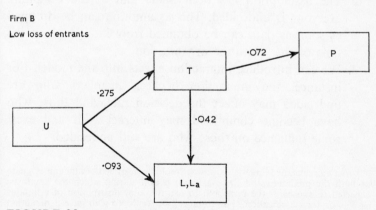

Firm B

Low loss of entrants

FIGURE 28 DECISION-PROCESS STRUCTURE FOR FIRMS A AND B
High values show high transition rate

decision stage, but also after having made a temporary commitment, which suggests that there may be something unattractive within the organization itself.

This is perhaps as far as we can go at present by means of input-output techniques. The present model makes it possible to predict, for each point in time, how many entrants will be undecided, how many temporarily committed, how many permanently committed, and how many have decided to leave. However, to test these implications we shall need to wait until a way can be found to follow a sufficiently large group of entrants over a period of time. The type of information needed is how many entrants at any one time are still undecided and how many have come to the stage where they consider themselves to be permanently committed to the organization.[1]

With the help of data of this type it would be possible to go further and test the implications of more complex models which are obtained by dropping one or all of the following simplifying assumptions:

1. The present model is stated in terms of net flows. It would be possible to investigate models which permit backward flow, where, for instance, a person who has become temporarily committed becomes again undecided.
2. The assumption has been made that at the beginning everyone is undecided. This assumption can be dropped as soon as data can be obtained from individuals at the time of entry into the organization.
3. We can introduce interaction effects into the model. For instance, the interaction between members who are undecided may affect the decision rate, and those who have become committed may interact with and exert some influence on those who are still undecided.

[1] In a more detailed interview study, it would be possible to obtain an estimate of both the minimum and the maximum period during which the employee expected to stay with the firm, and to use the joint distribution of estimates as a basis for classification. For instance, an employee who gave a minimum estimate of two weeks and a maximum estimate of three weeks would be one who had decided to leave.

Models that include interaction processes are easy to set up on an analogue computer. However, the non-linear differential equations that result present formidable, and so far unsolved, mathematical problems.

It appears likely that progress made in the analysis of non-linear systems may in time provide greater insight into organizational dynamics, and also into what appear to be structurally similar processes in the field of psychology, such as retention and the structure of memory organization.[1]

[1] For a further development and extension of this model, see Bartholomew (1967).

AFTERWORD

THIS VOLUME has described four different types of technique that have been developed for the study of single cases and has demonstrated how these can be used to examine both the structure and the evolution of behavioural organizations. The book represents a further development of a theory and methodology first presented in *Autonomous Group Functioning* (Herbst, 1962). The results obtained show that every person and every group has the characteristics of a unique behavioural universe with its own laws and measurement scales. The formulation of a general behaviour theory is found to be possible at the level of a set of basic postulates from which the possible networks of behaviour principles that can evolve can be derived.

It is shown that the nature of individual and group tasks—specifically, their physical and technological characteristics—determines the potential range of principles in terms of which a behavioural organization can operate. In a companion volume on socio-technical theory and design this approach will be taken further and applied to the problem of organizational design.

Main objectives of the companion volume are to extend the theoretical foundation for socio-technical studies and to examine the conditions for the emergence and development in Norway and other countries of non-hierarchical forms of organization in industry, research and education. It begins by discussing the different types of model that can be applied to the integration of psychological and physical concepts to provide a basis for the socio-technical study of organizations and for the development of principles for the socio-technical design of organizations. A major aim is to discover types of organization able to survive and function effectively under the present conditions of rapid technological change. A detailed case-

233

study carried out in the shipping industry shows that this problem is not soluble unless policy decisions with respect to technological changes are directively correlated and consistent with policy decisions with respect to societal and social organizational changes. At the same time, it becomes necessary to build into existing organizations the capacity for continuous learning.

The transition from a society that has evolved adjusting itself to technological changes to one that has the potential capacity for planning and creating its own future implies a fundamental transformation, not only of society itself, but also of the requirements for theoretical and applied science and of the relationship of man both to himself and to his environment.

BIBLIOGRAPHY

ALLPORT, F. H. (1937). Teleonomic Description in the Study of Personality. *Charact. and Pers.* **5**, 202–214.

ARGYLE, M., and DELIN, P. (1965). Non-universal Laws of Socialization. *Hum. Relat.* **18**, 77–86.

ASHBY, W. R. (1947). Principles of the Self-organizing Dynamic System. *J. gen. Psychol.* **37**, 125–128.

ASHBY, W. R. (1952). *Design for a Brain.* New York: Wiley.

ASHBY, W. R. (1962). Principles of the Self-organizing System. In H. V. Foerster and G. W. Zopf (eds.), *Principles of Self-organization.* Oxford: Pergamon Press.

BAKAN, D. (1954). A Generalization of Sidman's Results on Group and Individual Functions and a Criterion. *Psychol. Bull.* **51**, 63–64.

BAKAN, D. (1967). *On Method: Toward a Reconstruction of Psychological Investigation.* San Francisco: Jossey-Bass.

BANDURA, A., LIPSHER, D. H., and MILLER, P. A. (1960). Psychotherapist's Approach Avoidance Reactions to Patients' Expression of Hostility. *J. consult. Psychol.* **24**, 1–8.

BARKER, R., DEMBO, T., and LEWIS, K. (1941). Frustration and Regression. In *Studies in Topological and Vector Psychology II. Univ. Ia. Stud. Child Welf.* **20**.

BARTH, F. (1963). *The Role of the Entrepreneur in Social Change in Northern Norway.* Bergen and Oslo: Norwegian Universities Press.

BARTH, F. (1966). *Models of Social Organization.* Royal Anthropological Institute Occasional Papers No. 23.

BARTHOLOMEW, D. J. (1959). Note on the Measurement and Prediction of Labour Turnover. *J. roy. statist. Soc. (Series A)* **122**.

BARTHOLOMEW, D. J. (1967). *Stochastic Models for Social Processes.* New York: Wiley.

BAVELAS, A. (1948). A Mathematical Model for Group Structures. *Appl. Anthrop.* **1**, 16–30.

BECK, S. (1966). Preliminary Results of Interaction Code on Seven Couples. (Mimeo.) Cambridge, Mass.: Harvard Medical School, Family Research Unit.

BERTALANFFY, L. VON (1950). The Theory of Open Systems in Physics and Biology. *Science* **3**, 25–29.

Q

BERTALANFFY, L. VON (1951). Theoretical Models in Biology and Psychology. *J. Pers.* **20**, 24–38.

BEURLE, R. L. (1962). Functional Organization in Random Networks. In H. V. Foerster and G. W. Zopf (eds.), *Principles of Self-organization.* Oxford: Pergamon Press.

BEVAN, W., and MAIER, R. A. (1958). Emotional Tension and Performance. *J. Pers.* **26**, 330–336.

BLOCK, J., and MARTIN, P. (1955). Predicting the Behaviours of Children under Frustration. *J. abnorm. soc. Psychol.* **51**, 281–285.

BOTT, ELIZABETH (1957). *Family and Social Network.* London: Tavistock Publications.

BRIANT, D. T. (1965). A Survey of the Development of Manpower Planning Policies. *Brit. J. indus. Relat.* **3**, 279–290.

BRIDGEMAN, P. W. (1931). *Dimensional Analysis.* London: Oxford University Press; New Haven, Conn.: Yale University Press.

BRONOWSKI, J. (1959). *Science and Human Values.* New York: Harper.

CARTWRIGHT, D., and HARARY, F. (1956). Structural Balance: A Generalization of Heider's Theory. *Psychol. Rev.* **63**, 277–293.

CHASSAN, J. B. (1960). Statistical Inference and the Single Case in Clinical Design. *Psychiatry* **23**, 173–184.

CHEIN, I. (1954). The Environment as a Determinant of Behaviour. *J. soc. Psychol.* **39**, 115–127.

CHURCHMAN, C. W., and EMERY, F. E. (1966). On Various Approaches to the Study of Organizations. In *Operational Research and the Social Sciences.* London: Tavistock Publications.

COLEMAN, J. S. (1964). *Introduction to Mathematical Sociology.* Glencoe, Ill.: Free Press.

COLEMAN, J. S., KATZ, E., and MENZEL, H. (1966). *Medical Innovation: A Diffusion Study.* Indianapolis: Bobbs-Merrill.

DAVIS, L. E. (1962). The Effects of Automation on Job Design. *Indus. Relat.* **2** (1).

DAVIS, L. E. (1966). The Design of Jobs. *Indus. Relat.* **6**, 21–45.

EMERY, F. E. (1959). *Characteristics of Socio-technical Systems.* Tavistock Institute Doc. 527.

EMERY, F. E. (1963). *In Search of Some Principles of Persuasion.* Tavistock Institute Doc. T 10.

EMERY, F. E. (1966). *Report on a Theoretical Study of Unit Operations.* Tavistock Institute Doc. 900.

EMERY, F. E., and TRIST, E. L. (1965). The Causal Texture of Organizational Environments. *Hum. Relat.* **18**, 21–32.

ERIKSON, E. (1959). Identity and the Life Cycle: Selected Papers. *Psychol. Issues* **1** (1).

FAULKNER, T. E. (1952). *Projective Geometry.* Edinburgh: Oliver & Boyd; New York: Interscience Publishers.

FLAMENT, C. (1963). *Applications of Graph Theory to Group Structure.* Englewood Cliffs, N.J.: Prentice-Hall.

FOGEL, L. J., *et al.* (1966). Intelligent Decision Making through a Simulation of Evolution. *Behav. Sci.* **11** (4).

FRANK, F. (1953). Untersuchungen über den Zusammenbruch von Feldmausplagen (Microtus arvalis). *Zool. Jahrb.* **82**, 95–136.

GALTUNG, J. (1967). *Theory and Methods of Social Research.* Oslo: Universitetsforlaget; New York: Columbia University Press.

GLUCKMAN, M. (ed.) (1962). *Essays on the Ritual of Social Relations.* Manchester: Manchester University Press.

GOLDSMITH, M., and MACKAY, A. (eds.) (1964). *The Science of Science: Society in the Technological Age.* London: Souvenir Press.

GREENWOOD, M. (1918). *A Report on the Causes of Wastage of Labour in Munition Factories employing Women.* London: Medical Research Committee, Special Report No. 16.

HEDBERG, M. (1962). The Turnover of Labour in Industry, an Actuarial Study. *Acta. Sociol.* **5** (3), 129–143.

HEIDER, F. (1959; originally 1926). Thing and Medium. *Psychol. Issues Monograph* **3**, 1–34.

HEIDER, F. (1946). Attitudes and Cognitive Organization. *J. Psychol.* **21**, 107–112.

HERBST, P. G. (1949). The Force Field Hypothesis and the Method of Continuous Differentiation. Research Report, Dept. of Psychology Library, University of Melbourne.

HERBST, P. G. (1952). The Measurement of Family Relationships. *Hum. Relat.* **5**, 3–35, and *Bulletin de Psychologie*, 1953, **7**, 566–588.

HERBST, P. G. (1953). Analysis and Measurement of a Situation: The Child in the Family. *Hum. Relat.* **6**, 113–140.

HERBST, P. G. (1954a). Family Living. Chapters 10–12 in O. A. Oeser and S. B. Hammond (eds.), *Social Structure and Personality in a City.* London: Routledge & Kegan Paul; New York: Macmillan.

HERBST, P. G. (1954b). Analysis of Social Flow Systems. *Hum. Relat.* **7**, 327–336.

HERBST, P. G. (1954c). Limits to a Firm's Control of Labour Turnover. *Nature* **173**, 1150.

HERBST, P. G. (1957a). Situation Dynamics and the Theory of Behaviour Systems. *Behav. Sci.* **2**, 13–28.

HERBST, P. G. (1957b). An Approach to the Measurement of the Level of Organization of Behaviour Systems. *Proceedings of the 15th International Congress of Psychology.* North Holland Publ. Co.

HERBST, P. G. (1957c). Measurement of Behaviour Structures by Means of Input-Output Data. *Hum. Relat.* **10**, 335–346.

HERBST, P. G. (1961). A Theory of Simple Behaviour Systems I & II. *Hum. Relat.* **14**, 71–94, 193–240.

HERBST, P. G. (1962). *Autonomous Group Functioning: An Exploration in Behaviour Theory and Measurement.* London: Tavistock Publications.

HERSHKOVITZ, A. (1954). Interpersonal Agreement and Disagreement on Objects and Values: A Preliminary Study. Unpublished Doctoral Dissertation, University of Kansas.

HILL, R., and HANSEN, D. A. (1960). The Identification of Conceptual Frameworks Utilised in Family Studies. *Marriage and Family Living* **22**, 299–311.

HUNTER, G. H., and KITTRELL, J. R. (1966). Evolutionary Operations: A Review. *Technometrics* **8**, 389–397.

IPSEN, D. C. (1960). *Units, Dimension and Dimensionless Numbers.* New York: McGraw-Hill Paperbacks.

JORDAN, N. (1963). Allocation of Functions between Man and Machines in Automated Systems. *J. appl. Psychol.* **47** (3), 161–165.

JORDAN, N. (1965). On Cognitive Balance. (Mimeo.) University of Kansas.

JOHNSEN, E. (1965). Organisationsteoriernes specifikke bidrag til modelegenskaber for styring af meneske-maskin systemer. *Sociologisk Forskning* **2** (2).

JOHNSEN, E. (1968). *Studies in Multi-objective Decision Models.* Lund: Studentlitteratur.

KAHN, R. L. (1956). The Prediction of Productivity. *J. soc. Issues.* **12**, 41–49.

KAPP, K. W. (1954). Economics and the Behavioural Sciences. *Cyclos* **7**, 205–225.

LANE, K. F., and ANDREW, J. E. (1955). A Method of Labour Turnover Analysis. *J. roy. statist. Soc. (Series A)* **118**.

LEWIN, K. (1936). *Principles of Topological Psychology*. New York and London: McGraw-Hill.

LEWIN, K. (1947). Frontiers in Group Dynamics. *Hum. Relat.* **1**, 2–38.

LEWIN, K. (1951). *Field Theory in Social Science*. New York: Harper; London: Tavistock Publications, 1952.

LUCE, R. D. (1959). On the Possible Psycho-physical Laws. *Psychol. Rev.* **66**, 81–95.

MARCUSE, H. (1964). *One Dimensional Man*. London: Routledge & Kegan Paul.

MAREK, J. (1967). Technological Development, Organization and Interpersonal Relations. *Acta Sociol.* **10** (3–4), 224–257.

MEHRABIAN, A. (1966). Attitudes in relation to the Forms of Communicator-Object Relationship in Spoken Communications. *J. Pers.* **34**, 80–93.

MILLS, T. M. (1952). A Method of Content Analysis of Small Groups. Unpublished Doctoral Dissertation, Harvard University.

MISHLER, E. G., and WAXLER, N. E. (1964). *An Experimental Study of Families with Schizophrenics: Interaction Codebook*. (Progress Report.) Harvard University.

MORENO, J. L. (1934). *Who Shall Survive?* Washington D.C.: Nervous and Mental Diseases Publ. Co.

NEUBECK, G. (1964). The Decision to Marry while in College. In E. Grønseth (ed.), Approaches to the Study of the Decision to Marry. *Acta Sociol.* **8**, 112.

PAASCHE, T. (1965, 1966). Development and Stability of Scientific and Engineering Interests and their Translation into Career Decisions. Tavistock Institute Docs. T 548, 567, 795.

PASK, G. (1962). The Simulation of Learning and Decision-making Behaviour. In C. A. Muses (ed.), *Aspects of the Theory of Artificial Intelligence*. New York: Plenum Press.

PRICE, D. J. DE SOLLA (1962). *Science since Babylon*. New Haven, Conn.: Yale University Press.

RAPOPORT, RHONA (1964). The Transition from Engagement to Marriage. In E. Grønseth (ed.), Approaches to the Study of the Decision to Marry. *Acta Sociol.* **8**, 112.

RAPOPORT, RHONA (1967). The Study of Marriage as a Critical Transition for Personality and Family Development. In P. Lomas (ed.), *The Predicament of the Family*. London: Hogarth.

239

RAPOPORT, R. N. (1956). Oscillations and Sociotherapy. *Hum. Relat.* **9**, 357–374.

RAPOPORT, R. N., and RAPOPORT, RHONA (1965). Work and Family in Contemporary Society. *Amer. sociol. Rev.* **30**, 381–394.

RICE, A. K. (1951). An Examination of the Boundaries of Part Institutions. *Hum. Relat.* **4**, 393–400.

RICE, A. K., HILL, J. M. M., and TRIST, E. L. (1950). The Representation of Labour Turnover as a Social Process. *Hum. Relat.* **3**, 349–372.

RICE, A. K., and TRIST, E. L. (1952). Institutional and Sub-institutional Determinants of Change in Labour Turnover. *Hum. Relat.* **5**, 347–371.

ROSENMAN, S. (1955). Changes in the Representation of Self, Others and Interrelationships in Client-Centered Therapy. *J. Counselling Psychol.* **2**, 271.

RUSSELL, W. M. S., MEAD, A. P., and HAYES, J. S. (1954). A Basis for the Quantitative Study of the Structure of Behaviour. *Behaviour* **6**, 154.

SCHRÖDINGER, E. (1958). *Mind and Matter*. Cambridge: Cambridge University Press.

SIDMAN, M. (1952). A Note on Functional Relationships obtained from Group Data. *Psychol. Rev.* **49**, 261–269.

SILCOCK, H. (1954). The Phenomenon of Labour Turnover. *J. roy. statist. Soc.* (*Series A*) **117**, 429–440.

SIMON, H. A. (1954). Some Strategic Considerations in the Construction of Social Science Models. Chapter 8 in P. F. Lazarsfeld (ed.), *Mathematical Thinking in Social Sciences*. Glencoe, Ill.: Free Press.

SOMMERHOFF, G. (1960). *Analytical Biology*. London: Oxford University Press.

SPECTOR, A. J. (1956). Expectations, Fulfilment and Morale. *J. abnorm. soc. Psychol.* **52**, 51–56.

STANSFIELD, R. G. (1951). Levels of Expectation in Productivity. *Occup. Psychol.* **25**, 25–34.

TRIST, E. L., and BAMFORTH, K. W. (1951). Some Social and Psychological Consequences of the Longwall Method of Coal Getting. *Hum. Relat.* **4**, 3–38.

TRIST, E. L., HIGGIN, G. W., MURRAY, H., and POLLOCK, A. B. (1963). *Organizational Choice*. London: Tavistock Publications.

INDEX

INDEX

action level
  of behaviour system, 48
  of group, 48
activity, definition of, 48
affect, 149
  prediction of direction of, 194
  prediction of rank order of, 196
affect arousal, potential for, 215
affect balance, 179–82, 189
affect categories, 154
affect control, 215
affect initiation and response patterns, 179–80
affect rank order, 200, 201, 206
affect system, meta-stable, 174
affect trajectories, 172–82
Allport, F. H., 235
Andrew, J. E., 219, 239
anxiety, 11, 39, 41, 50, 94, 103, 107, 109, 111–14, 119, 122, 125, 126, 130, 131, 133, 139
  as function of work effort required and expected performance level, 138–9
Argyle, M., 235
Ashby, W. R., 235
attitudinal balance, 191
attitudinal configurations, 191
attitudinal relationship, 189
attributed personal affect, 150

Bakan, D., 235
balance
  conditions of, 49, 51
  see also cognitive balance
Bamforth, K. W., 240
Bandura, A., 180n, 235
Barker, R., 235
Barth, F., 235
Bartholomew, D. J., 220, 231n, 235
Bartholomew function, 220–2, 226
Bavelas, A., 161, 235
Beck, S., 235

behaviour, aim direction of, 30
behavioural laws, 4–5
  nature of, 47–55
  network of, 54
  range of possible, 3–13
behavioural networks, 119
behavioural phenomena, search for workable representation of, 4
behavioural sciences
  assumptions taken over from classical physics, ix, xi, 3, 14–15
  present state of, 3
behavioural universes, xi, 8, 29, 55, 209, 233
behaviour principles, xiii, 15
  derivation of, 62–3
  networks of, 40, 62
  under conditions of outcome predictability, 59–84
behaviour system, 52–3
  action level of, 48
  basic concepts in, study of, 47–55
  cessation of, 53
  concepts that define functioning of, 93
  mode of functioning, 52
  simple, 24–5
  use of term, 47
behaviour theory
  breakdown of physicalist postulates in, 14–21
  generalized, 20–1, 22–34, 65
behaviour trajectories, 163
behaviour unit, 60
behaviour variables
  internal, 25, 29, 30, 62, 67, 89, 112
  relationships between, passim
  transactional, 25, 29, 30, 62, 68, 89, 113
Bertalanffy, L. von, 235
Beurle, R. L., 236
Bevan, W., 236
Block, J., 236

1